I0797627

FADED GLAMOUR
in the City

FADED GLAMOUR *in the City*

inspirational interiors
and beautiful homes

PEARL LOWE

with photography by
KATE MARTIN

CICO BOOKS

This book is dedicated to my husband Danny and our four children Daisy, Alfie, Frankie and Betty, who continually inspire me!

Photography Kate Martin
Additional photography Helena Christensen (pages 116–131)
Styling Alex Teal
Words Zia Mattocks
Endpapers Morton, Young & Borland Textiles
Senior designer Toni Kay
Editor Sophie Devlin
Head of production Patricia Harrington
Senior commissioning editor Annabel Morgan
Art director Sally Powell
Creative director Leslie Harrington

Published in 2025 by CICO Books. An imprint of Ryland Peters & Small
20–21 Jockey's Fields
London WC1R 4BW
and
1452 Davis Bugg Road
Warrenton, NC 27589

www.rylandpeters.com
Email: euregulations@rylandpeters.com

10 9 8 7 6 5 4 3 2 1

ISBN 978-1-80065-467-9

A CIP record for this book is available from the British Library.

Library of Congress CIP data has been applied for.

Printed and bound in Slovenia.

The authorised representative in the EEA is Authorised Rep Compliance Ltd., Ground Floor. 71 Lower Baggot Street, Dublin, D01 P593, Ireland
www.arccompliance.com

CONTENTS

RIGHT **I love creating displays of meaningful items on shelves. They are a delight to me and enhance any space. Arranging pieces in a cohesive colour scheme creates a harmonious look, beautifully illustrated by this stunning display of lace, lamps and figurines at one of my favourite shops, Muirshin Durkin.**

OPPOSITE **This wonderful emporium on Golborne Road in Notting Hill has something new to catch the eye on every visit. It specializes in antique furniture from the 18th to the mid 19th century, as well as vintage clothing. The Made by Muirshin collection of custom crafted items includes faux bamboo furniture and velvet mirrors.**

INTRODUCTION

I get itchy feet. I don't know what it is, but ever since I was young, I have always loved a change. It's just in my nature. My husband Danny always says I have Romani blood because I am descended from ancient Eastern European travelling communities. That might play a part in it. Or maybe my restlessness has something to do with my recent ADHD diagnosis (most probable).

Or it could simply be an unwavering desire to create, decorate and re-decorate homes, to make them look and feel beautiful. In the same way that a musician or an artist might feel quite lost and unfulfilled without an outlet for their creativity, I feel rather directionless and unsatisfied when I am not realizing my visions, or working on or towards an aesthetic project of some kind.

When it comes to the creation of this book, I guess the timing was right for its conception. Danny also loves a change – we had put our house by the sea in East Sussex up for sale and were plotting our next move with the business. We had begun musing over what it might be like to spend a bit of time back in London.

It's been 20 years since we moved out of our beloved Camden townhouse and into the Somerset countryside, and I still believe that leaving London when we did was the right decision. We brought the kids up in Somerset and made many lifelong friends there. We've enjoyed the beautiful green spaces and the slower, friendlier way of life. We both knew that we didn't want to up sticks and leave Somerset as a base, but we just needed a bit of, I don't know... action?

Most of our kids have now flown the nest and we are new grandparents to our eldest daughter Daisy's sweet baby girl. They live in London, as does my mother, who although still as active as ever, is well into her eighties and needs more of my attention now. The timing was right, and it was London we fancied.

When the sale of our beach house went through in September 2024, I began looking at properties in London. The creative juices started to flow and I wondered if *Faded Glamour in the City* might be a cool addition to my previous two books, *Faded Glamour* and *Faded Glamour by the Sea*.

MIRROR

OPPOSITE AND ABOVE
Laurence Roche, the owner of Muirshin Durkin, travels all over the world to source the antique furniture and decorative items that he restores, reworks and sells in the shop, alongside his sustainably crafted pieces. He has such a good eye that I know I will love whatever he has in stock, so I visit as often as I can for inspiration. It's not unusual for me to pop in for a minute and go home with a treasure that I just had to snap up before someone else does!

I loved putting those two books together and felt that city-based interiors with a similar aesthetic would be the perfect subject for a third book. Because I have featured my own houses in the previous Faded Glamour books, I thought what fun it would be this time to do up and decorate a London flat and work on this new book at the same time.

After agreeing the plan with Danny, I initially leant towards East London in my house searches. I had never lived in that part of the city, but my dad grew up in the East End. I'm a big fan of the old Dickensian-style buildings around Brick Lane and Spitalfields Market, and I also love the multicultural vibrancy these areas have.

I found some great places online and had a look at a few, but I found that when we came into London from the West Country, the extra 45-minute trip across the capital was quite gruelling – there is just too much traffic! So we ended up looking at smaller flats that were just about in our budget in West London. Eventually, as if it were waiting for us, we found our wonderful little hidden gem in Notting Hill, just off Portobello Road.

I have always had a great love affair with this particular neighbourhood, mainly because of its historic street market – the vintage clothes, the antiques, the food and the buzz of people is so intoxicating. I used to get the tube to the market religiously every Friday, from my teenage years right up until Danny and I left London. The daily hustle and bustle of Portobello is like some kind of Mardi Gras. After all those years in the serenity of the countryside, I thought the sheer volume of people on the streets might freak me out.

ABOVE LEFT, ABOVE RIGHT AND OPPOSITE **The basement of the shop is filled with a fantastic selection of quirky objects, ceramics, figurines and glassware. Everything is displayed in pretty pink pigeonhole shelving. This gives some kind of order to an eclectic mix of items and makes it easy to visualize how things might work in the home. It's a great little shop to mooch around, and it's very hard to walk out without buying something.**

Instead, I've been happily padding around, usually with my trusty dog Doris beside me, down Portobello Road, on through the market and up to Golborne Road to have a snoop around. I rarely come home empty-handed, as there is always a new treasure to be found.

I also love living in the centre of everything again. The freedom of being able to hop on a bus or the Underground for a few stops to visit a gallery, go to the theatre or to see my son playing in his band, or just to meet friends or family for lunch, fills me with joy.

Working on this book over the past few months has been so fantastic, as it has allowed me to fall in love with city living all over again. Travelling around with my team of talented women, shooting all of these wonderful homes that feature in this book – everything from a five-storey townhouse to a bijou flat, to an artist's studio and even a narrowboat – has given me a new lease of life for city living.

Being in London now feels like a brand new experience. It's amazing to see how much the city has changed over the past 20 years. You could barely get a pizza delivered when I last lived there, but now everything is at your fingertips. So, until the next time I get those itchy feet...I love London Town!

Lots of love, *Pearl xx*

When Danny and I decided to move back to London, all but one of our children having flown the nest, we began looking in East London for a small house that would be big enough for the two of us and our youngest daughter Betty. I had envisaged something akin in style, though smaller in scale, to our beloved house in Camden, North London that we sold in 2005, when we upped sticks to fulfil our dreams of raising our children in the countryside. When our initial searches proved fruitless, we began to look further afield, which is how we ended up in West London, a stone's throw from Portobello Road.

MY FADED GLAMOUR *in the City*

OPPOSITE **Warm, dusky pinks and reds make the seating area feel so tranquil. My dog Doris loves to soak up the sun on the red velvet sofa from Soho Home, among cushions from Preen by Thornton Bregazzi and Sera of London. On the wall hang two paintings by Lorena Lohr. I've had the Italian table for 15 years – I was planning to sell it, but changed my mind because it works so well here.**

ABOVE RIGHT **The pocket-sized entrance hall is both pretty and practical, with a shelf for keys. I love traditional cast-iron radiators and always paint them the same colour as the walls. The vintage standard lamp was an eBay find.**

When this property came up for sale – coincidentally, just around the corner from my very first flat, where I lived more than 30 years ago – I went to view it on my own. I thought, I'll just look at it, but I don't think it's going to be right. It is tiny, at only 880sq ft/81.75sq m, but it's got high ceilings and is unusual for a London flat because it doesn't have a shared entrance. As soon as I stepped inside, I thought: 'Oh, wow!' I was taken aback by the height of the ceilings and the feeling of grandeur. The owner had used the space as a therapy room since 1995, so it felt like a very healing space. It hadn't been decorated for years, and had all the original period features that I love, but it needed work, and that's exactly what I wanted.

I've never done up a flat before, so this has been a new challenge for me. Somehow a house is more forgiving, as there are more rooms to try things out and fit things in, whereas with a flat you have to make the space work hard and think about every little detail.

Originally, I had grand plans to divide up the open-plan living space, which stretches from the front to the back of the building, using a set of beautiful double doors, and to make the back part, with its soaring ceiling, into our bedroom. I thought it would make a fabulously romantic space, complete with an antique bed and freestanding bathtub. What is now our bedroom could have been a cute little kitchen, and the bathroom would have become a spacious shower room. However, Danny was adamant that we shouldn't reconfigure it that way and I lost the argument.

What we did agree on was that we didn't want it to look too much like a traditional kitchen, as it's part of the main space that you first walk into, but more like a bar or diner – fun and glamorous. We always work closely with deVOL to design our kitchens and were fortunate enough to do so here, too. The cabinets (finished in Farrow & Ball's Mizzle), sink, appliances, marble-topped butcher's table and bar stools are all from there.

OPPOSITE **I wanted this flat to celebrate women, so I've added many items that bring softness and femininity. The mantel, painted to match the walls, displays ostrich feathers, an angel figurine from Etsy, a Fornasetti candle and a glass dome of cards depicting naked women. The velvet cushion reminds me of a flower, with its playful 'stamen' in the form of a tassel.**

PAGES 14–15 AND ABOVE **I've collected antique French lace panels for years. They look so romantic hung at these tall windows and I love how they filter the light. I couldn't resist buying the beautiful lamp and the mustard velvet sofa from Muirshin Durkin, even though we didn't have a place for them at the time. I got them out of storage, as I knew they would be just right here. The glamorous shell cushion is by Sera of London. The Theodore velvet armchairs are from Soho Home and so is the Art Deco-style drinks cabinet – I'd been coveting it for a while and it's perfect for storing my collection of vintage glasses.**

The worktop is a stunning greyish green quartz with brown and red veins running through it, which we sourced from a great supplier in Frome, Somerset. We used one of my antique French lace curtains to screen the open shelves, a pair of antique lights from the cabin at our beach house and some gorgeous mirrored tiles from Fired Earth that make a unique splashback and add a decadent touch. I filled the shelves and surfaces with my favourite decorative objects – floral pictures, nudes and portraits of women, ceramics, glass bottles, taxidermy and feathers. I'm a maximalist through and through, and ever-changing displays bring me such joy.

Much to Danny's dismay, I insisted on tearing up the engineered-wood flooring, as I love the character and texture that old floorboards lend to a space. One day when he wasn't there I asked the builders to pull it up, and underneath were these beautiful floorboards. They were, however, a rather unsightly shade of orange and it took several weeks to install the required insulation, re-lay the floorboards and sand and stain them a rich dark brown – quite a palaver, but totally worth the effort.

We bought the flat in November and making decorating decisions during the winter months definitely influenced the colour palette. We've gone for rich, soft, warm tones that feel cosy and cocooning – shades of brown, pink, green, russet, red and mustard. We had set our hearts on painting the walls of the main living space in Potted Shrimp by Farrow & Ball, a lovely shade of blush pink, but after applying just one coat it looked so brown that we had to repaint it in the lighter shade of Setting Plaster, which brings a warm glow to the room. It looks stunning against the brown wood floor, the Mizzle-painted units and woodwork/trim, and the rich, spicy shades of our velvet-covered sofas and chairs from Soho Home. I absolutely love using vintage rugs to add colour, pattern and softness underfoot, and I found a couple of fabulous ones on Etsy that tie all the colours together.

The bedrooms are snug and enveloping spaces, inviting a restful night's sleep. I designed our bedroom around the gorgeous antique emperor-size French bed, which turned out to be a bit bigger than I had anticipated and almost didn't fit. It's dressed with the softest pink bed linen from Piglet in Bed and a beautiful bedspread that I bought from Helen Parker, the Creative Director at deVOL. The walls are painted in chocolaty Salon Drab, again from Farrow & Ball, and I edged them with a wonderful bobble trim that I found in Shepherd's Bush Market. It's really pretty and unexpected, and finishes off the room perfectly.

The standout feature of my daughter's room is the pair of stunning bell-shaped pink glass wall lights from Rothschild & Bickers. As soon as I spotted them, with their playful fringing, I knew they would work well. They're such beautiful jewel-like objects and they make the room feel magical. We originally painted the walls pink, but it felt a bit boring, so I had them lined with Mulberry Home's striking Somerton Stripe wallpaper in russet, and I love the depth that it brings to the space. The bed is from Soho Home and I trimmed it with a vintage frill to give it a more feminine touch. I found some curtains in a flea market that fit the colour scheme and finished them with a tassel trim. That's the joy of collecting textiles – there's always the perfect trim to add when you need it.

The little shower room next to Betty's room has a concealed cupboard recessed into the wall behind the mirror. It's a brilliantly practical storage solution in a small space and means that all her clutter is hidden from view.

ABOVE LEFT **This French cabinet is affectionately known as 'the beast', as I misread its dimensions when I bought it online. It holds everything – printer, paper, glasses and paperwork. Displayed on top of it are my portraits of women by the mid-century French artist Louis Dazza, together with a nude and a retro radio.**

ABOVE RIGHT **Shelves are such a great way to decorate a wall. On display here are some of my treasured glass bottles, paintings and ostrich feathers. The little lamp below was an eBay find.**

OPPOSITE **We wanted the kitchen to feel like a cool bar where we could have parties. The deVOL cabinets are painted in Farrow & Ball's Mizzle, which works so well with the Setting Plaster walls and dark wood floor. Glamorous elements include the marble-topped butcher's table and bar stools, the antique lighting and lace panels, the quartz worktop and the mirrored tiles from Fired Earth.**

SMEG

The walls are covered in a spongeable wallpaper by Jean Monro called Cambridge Rose. It's a charming pattern of pink rose sprigs and lilac rosehips, like a rambling climber in a country garden. The shell-pink floor tiles were laid when I was away and were meant to be cream, but I think they look sweet, so I decided to keep them.

We completely gutted the main bathroom and replaced the window with star-patterned frosted glass. The centrepiece is the gorgeous tub from BC Designs. It's a huge 180cm/71in and I love it. I was away when it was delivered and the builder FaceTimed me saying, 'The bathtub is too big!' I said, 'It needs to fit, you've got to make it work.' I've hung romantic white drapes around it, which I bought at Shepton Mallet flea market. The vintage-style marble sink is from deVOL – I've been coveting it for a very long time. We chose pink-and-white glazed rectangular tiles from Bert & May to create vertical stripes that accentuate the high ceiling. Both the walls and woodwork/trim are painted chalky pink – it's so pretty and feels a bit Parisian. There's something about a pink bathroom that is just so restful and uplifting.

OPPOSITE AND LEFT **Bringing in pretty elements such as decorative ceramics, vintage pictures, a beaded lamp and antique lights has elevated the kitchen from a purely functional space and given it so much personality. The ceramic cat by Liv & Dom was a gift from my daughter.**

ABOVE **I found the dining table at Shepton Mallet flea market and love its rustic surface – it was just a little too low, so I asked a friend to add some extra height to its legs. The bamboo chairs have been collected over the years. The pencil nude drawings are dated 1911 and were bought at an auction in Somerset; I thought they would be perfect for my 'celebrating women' theme.**

I brought a lot of my cherished items from our beach house in Sussex to furnish the flat, but it's been a challenge to edit our belongings and find what will work here. I'm constantly changing things around and taking pieces back to Somerset, then returning again with a car filled to the brim with other bits and bobs.

I'm a great believer that if you see something you love, you should buy it, even if you don't have a space for it yet. By the same token, you can't rush things when you're decorating with vintage. You have to learn the art of patience, as you never know when you will stumble across the perfect piece for your home.

I've always said that Danny and I get itchy feet – we like to move on every couple of years, but for now, this glamorous little London bolthole is ideal for us. I want to spend all my time here. It's become my happy place in the beating heart of one of my favourite parts of the city.

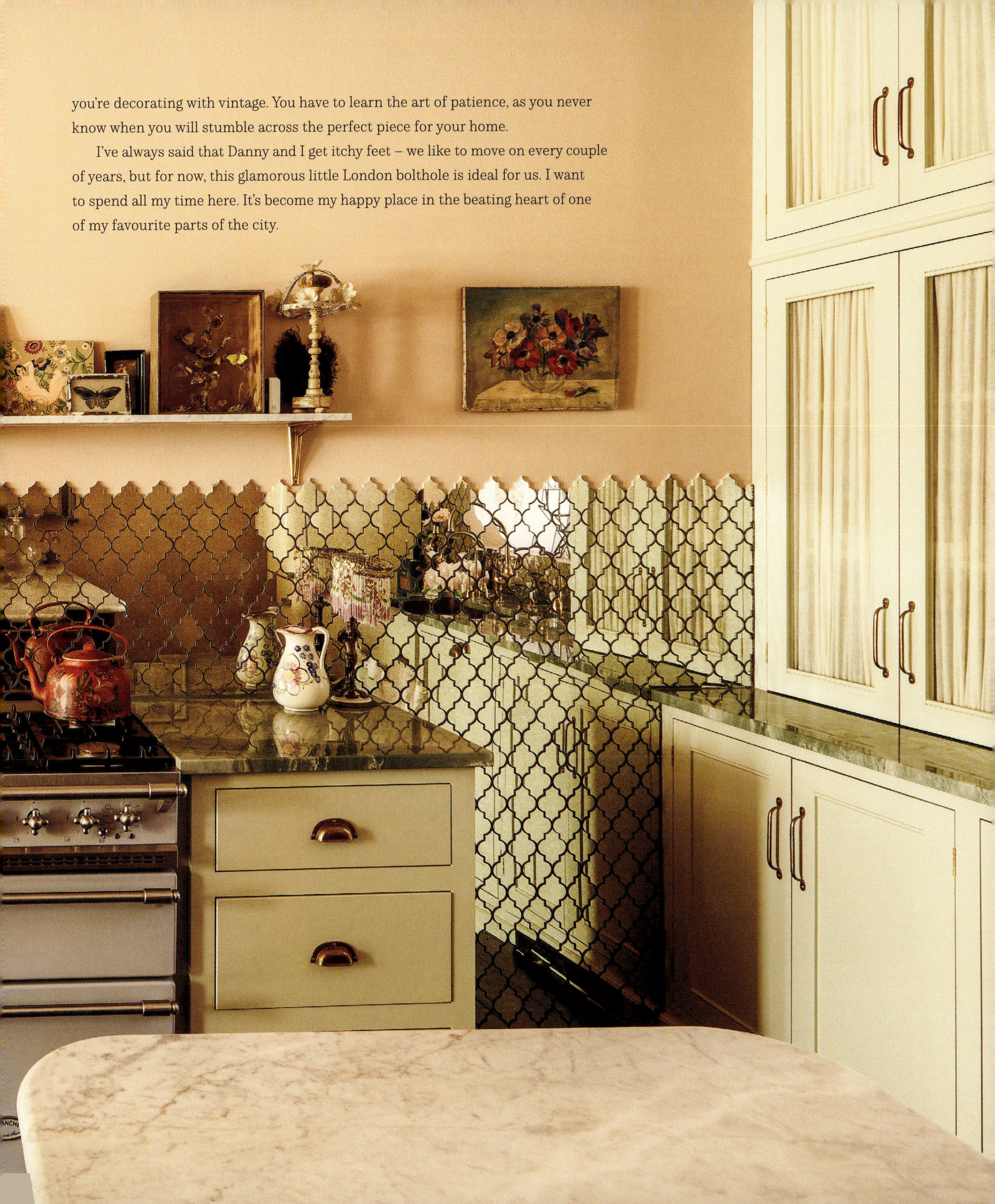

PAGES 22–23 The Deco Glass tiles from Fired Earth that we used as a splashback behind the cooker/stove and sink have the finish of an antique mirror and create such a pretty and glamorous look. They define the kitchen space and reflect light. The shelf of pictures and trinkets brings so much character and I think the wall would look really bare without it. Danny complains that our art is worth nothing, but I love my collections of vintage florals, portraits and nudes.

LEFT The hall leading to the bedrooms is painted in Mizzle by Farrow & Ball, which is a great neutral. The stair runner is by Roger Oates and the floor lamp I found years ago at a flea market.

OPPOSITE I planned the bedroom decor around the beautiful French bed, which has my favourite memory-foam Tempur mattress and the softest pink linen from Piglet in Bed. I painted the walls in Salon Drab by Farrow & Ball. The look is softened by the dainty bedspread, lace curtains and antique chandelier. I found the Venetian glass mirror at Kempton antiques market.

PAGE 26 I've collected vintage clothing for years – this blue chiffon dress is from Rockstar Boudoir. The decorative trunk, useful for spare bed linen, is from Shepton Mallet flea market. I love the wooden beaded curtain that hangs in the entrance to the bedroom, as it adds another layer of pattern and texture.

PAGE 27 The sage-coloured lace curtains were handmade and embellished with a dusky pink bobble trim by the curtain maker Tori Murphy. A Florentine gilded bedside table/nightstand, one of a pair, holds a vase of flowers and a candle from Penhaligon's. The adorable cherub wall lights were an eBay find.

PENHALIGON'S

ABOVE I've been waiting for the right place to use this pretty Cambridge Rose wallpaper by Jean Monro and decided it was the ideal choice for Betty's bathroom.

LEFT For a cocooning effect in this bedroom, the ceiling and woodwork/trim are painted in Eating Room Red by Farrow & Ball, to match the Somerton Stripe wallpaper from Mulberry Home. I found the damask curtains at a flea market and added the trim. The flapper dress brings a hint of romance.

ABOVE The vintage mirror with a mustard velvet frame is from Etsy. I love its whimsical decoupage.

RIGHT Early 20th-century mirrored furniture pieces like these bedside tables/nightstands are hard to find. They are perfectly paired with the elegant fringed glass wall lights from Rothschild & Bickers. Together with the velvet cushions, the textured bedspread from Toast and the vintage frill adorning the Soho Home bed, they create the ambience of a decadent boudoir. Comfort is ensured with another Tempur mattress and Pembroke Stripe linen from Piglet in Bed. The floral oil painting is from Muirshin Durkin.

"I'm a maximalist through and through, and ever-changing displays bring me such joy."

ABOVE **Pink is such a good colour in a bathroom: warm, uplifting and flattering. The chalky pink paint used on the walls and woodwork/trim was made up for me by Bert & May to match the tiles. I love gazing at a display of favourite objects while soaking in the tub – a wall without a decorative shelf looks unfinished and bare to me.**

RIGHT **The decorative etched mirror, from Lark Vintage in Frome, Somerset, used to hang in a bathroom at our house in Sussex. I love its unusual shape and felt it could carry off a jaunty ostrich feather. The wall lights are from Soho Home and work well with the deVOL marble-topped washstand/vanity.**

OPPOSITE **The other walls were clad in stripes of glazed Skinny Metro tiles from Bert & May. The Senator bathtub from BC Designs is a showstopper and only just fits the width of the room. The brass fittings bring a vintage feel. I bought the star-patterned drapes from Shepton Mallet flea market and the pendant lamp from Mary Hossack Antiques.**

In a wonderful riverside setting in Hammersmith, West London sits this imposing former convent dating back to the mid 17th century. The building has had many additions, alterations and uses, but for the past 20 years or so it has been home to the architect Dominic Warren, his wife Heather Alston and their six children.

GRANDEUR *in the City*

ABOVE RIGHT **The house is set back from the towpath and partially hidden by the garden. Heather found the gate at her parents' house and luckily it fitted the gap in the wall perfectly.**

OPPOSITE **The former chapel, now a dining space, features a dramatic glass door from one of Dominic's architectural projects. The artwork above is by the couple's friend Luke Elwes. The other pictures were discovered in the attic of their previous house.**

As well as being a family home, this spectacular and unique building is also hired out as a location house through Carol Hayes Management, which is how I first discovered it around five years ago on a photo shoot for *Stella* magazine with my daughter Daisy.

Having just released my first interiors book, *Faded Glamour*, I was disappointed that I hadn't come across the house in time to include it. The distressed walls, soaring ceilings and original architecture all summed up the narrative perfectly. So when I began writing this book, I knew I had to feature it.

With 10 bedrooms, amazing views over the River Thames and a mix of antique furniture and faded floral furnishings, it is one of the most beautiful houses I've ever walked into in London. It has so much character and its varied and colourful past feels almost tangible.

How Dominic and Heather came to be its custodians seems quite serendipitous. They were already familiar with the houses on the riverside at Hammersmith, as they lived nearby at the time and often enjoyed walks along the towpath. When a property brochure arrived in the mail one day, they were curious to see inside the former convent. 'We instantly fell in love with it and very quickly hatched a plan to buy it,' Heather says with a laugh.

They learned that the house had been built in stages from the 1640s, significantly altered in the 1700s and divided into two in the 1800s when the owner demolished a barn and built Kelmscott House next door, later owned by William Morris. It became a convent in around 1914 and the chapel was built in the 1930s. In the 1970s, with only a few remaining nuns in residence, it was sold to a housing association and used as a hostel for asylum seekers. When that was closed, it was taken over by squatters.

As a listed property, there were limitations on what work could be done, but the couple bought it with planning permission and listed building consent to convert it back to a house. Dominic says the biggest job was removing all the partitions that had been installed.

'In the process, we discovered layers of changes that had been made over the years.' Georgian and Victorian modernizations included 'installing lower ceilings, adding new flat surfaces over previously panelled walls, removing fire surrounds and even walling over cupboard spaces.'

The next task was to strip off the 20th-century lining paper and reveal the wonderful surfaces beneath. The layers of old paint and plaster not only bring textural and tonal interest, they are evidence of the building's rich heritage.

The character of the house is the result of a combination of these timeless surfaces, inherited furniture and art, along with new acquisitions made on their travels, including many from favourite haunts in Devon and Cornwall, where they also have a house. Venice is a beloved destination and Italian style in general has had a great influence on their aesthetic. Heather cites her mother and grandmother as big inspirations, too, both of whom 'had an art for making old things look lovely and turning the ordinary into something beautiful.'

One of Heather's great friends is the textile designer Kate Forman, whose gorgeous vintage-inspired floral prints in her characteristic soft but sophisticated colours can be seen all over the house. I'm a huge fan of faded florals, as they instantly add prettiness and softness to any space. Heather and I also share a love for interiors that are constantly evolving, where furniture and furnishings can be changed around or replaced to keep things fresh.

Heather says, 'I love layering, so that nothing is of the moment but is built up over years. Rooms develop as I find something new or add in special items given as presents by friends or especially my children.' She also loves seeing how the familiar spaces can be transformed for photo shoots: 'I enjoy seeing my home through other people's eyes.' She concludes, 'I'm incredibly lucky to be married to a brilliant architect, and together we've worked to bring out the magic of the house, to make it a joy to live in but without losing its essence and history.'

OPPOSITE **The two 18th-century etchings of columns by Giovanni Battista Piranesi were bought from Christie's on a whim but are perfect for this tall wall. The much-loved sofa belonged to Heather's grandmother. 'Now the seat has gone, so we are almost sitting on the floor,' she says.**

ABOVE **The staircase came from another job of Dominic's and the pillar is one of a pair from M Charpentier Antiques in Fulham. Dominic had seen them in the window and loved them. When they were delivered here for a photo shoot, it felt like fate. Heather recalls: 'We lost money on that shoot, but gained some beautiful pillars!'**

OPPOSITE **The kitchen walls, cabinets, refrigerator and dishwasher are all painted in Edward Bulmer colours, with the ceiling left bare. Hanging dried flowers from the garden add colour and texture, an idea inspired by Athena Duncan of Rebel Rebel Flowers. The wall tiles were handmade and painted by Douglas Watson Studio. Some are based on Delft patterns, others have the initials of the couple's children and their partners and a few are based on the 14th-century floor tiles in the Palais des Papes in Avignon, France.**

ABOVE **I love the simple shape of the alcove in this lobby, which has been defined in white, along with the decorative plasterwork above it, to make it stand out against the pale blue wall paint by Edward Bulmer. The picture and the carved chair were both inherited from Heather's mother.**

DISHOOM

ABOVE LEFT In such a vast house, there are endless opportunities to create whimsical areas with different personalities. This landing has a lovely view of the garden through the curved window, which has perfectly fitting shutters hidden behind the pillars. The chairs were inherited and the toy horse came from an antiques fair.

ABOVE RIGHT AND RIGHT The front hall is an amazing space with so many original architectural details. Heather says, 'It feels very special with the arches and mouldings – there are lion heads, skulls and flowers.' The wallpaper was originally put up for a shoot, and the bust is one of a pair bought in Penzance, Cornwall. 'We were looking for a chest of drawers/dresser, but these seemed more fun.'

OPPOSITE The parquet-style flooring is made up of pieces of wood about 5cm/2in thick and has the most wonderful patina from years of traffic. The sculptural wooden chair was inherited and the stunning orange velvet curtain was found in their previous house.

LEFT AND ABOVE **The spare room has eight arched doorways that are not all in use. Throughout the house, Heather has primarily used Farrow & Ball Cornforth White, Pavilion Gray and Lamp Room Gray. However, some of the walls here were left unpainted so that their texture can be appreciated. Heather found the heavy vintage suitcases in her parents' loft and loves the past stories that their embossed initials and luggage labels conjure up. The flower paintings by the early 20th-century Cornish artist Emma Bunt were bought at auction.**

CRANACH
REMBRANDT
Arthur Rackham
THE MOSQUE
CHURCHES
PALACES
FRA ANGELICO
TOWN HOUSES
GRIMM'S FAIRY TALES
CHARLES LAMB
WOMEN POETS
CASSELL
LOUIS XIV
ROB KESSELER UP CLOSE
MODERNISMO
ESSENTIAL HOUSEBOOK
Royal Navy
BRAZIL
REIGN OF GEORGE V
DECORATIVE ARTS
ART
LANDMARK
NEW YORK ARCHITECTURE
PIERO DELLA FRANCESCA

OPPOSITE AND RIGHT

Bookshelves built around the doorway frame the view into the spare room. The decorative painted bed came from a shop in Oakham, Rutland. The bedside tables/nightstands are two old sewing boxes that Heather painted with the intention of hand-painting flowers on top – a work in progress. The rosy bed linen is an old Cath Kidston design; Heather says that when Cath did a shoot in the house, she was amused to see several of her old patterns, including some she had designed for Ikea. The floral bedcover was a present from a friend and Heather likes the contrast in styles.

"The character of the house is the result of a combination of timeless surfaces, inherited furniture and art, along with new acquisitions made on their travels."

OPPOSITE **The stripped fireplace in the main bedroom came from a project of Dominic's and the gilt mirror was bought from an architect friend. The portraits of women by the fashion illustrator and artist David Downton were a 40th-birthday present from Dominic to Heather. The dried-flower cushions were from a shoot and the garland around the hare was a gift from the milliner Piers Atkinson.**

ABOVE LEFT AND LEFT **These two pairs of small antique paintings came from an art fair and look so effective hung on either side of the bed.**

ABOVE **Bedrooms that are large enough to include comfortable seating are such a luxury. This pretty antique sofa came from friends and has been re-covered in soft pink linen from Kate Forman. Above it is a print by the Scottish artist Bruce McLean.**

PAGES 46–47 **This is Heather's favourite room in the house and I can see why: it's a very special place with an incredible view of the river and wonderful light. The beautiful Italian bed takes centre stage. The double chest of drawers/dresser is from Penzance Antiques and the treasured teddy on top was given to Heather by a friend of her mother's when she was a child.**

LEFT **I love the simplicity of this understated bathroom with its white fittings from Lefroy Brooks. Touches of glamour and prettiness are added by the chandelier rescued from Heather's parents' loft, the octagonal mirror from a bric-a-brac stall, the antique chair from Roderick Butler in Honiton and the floral blind/shade from Kate Forman. A few well-chosen trinkets, such as the vases of flowers and the row of little glass bottles, can elevate a minimalist space.**

OPPOSITE **Tall windows fill the stairwell with natural light by day, and at night an antique chandelier twinkles overhead. The seating area is softened by the patterned rug and linen curtains in a floral design by Kate Forman. Heather's parents brought back the camel stool from Egypt in the 1960s. The large pictures on the right are a representation of dreams by Heather's friend, artist Jane Gifford. Opposite are framed designs for costumes for the ugly stepsisters in *Cinderella*.**

THE BLOOMSBURY LOOK
WENDY HITCHMOUGH
FLORA SOAMES · THE ONE DAY BOX

The West London home of designer and artist Susi Bellamy has proved to be the ideal canvas to showcase an exuberant mix of her wonderful textiles, wallpapers, homeware and art, curated to perfection with her expert eye and instinct for combining colour and pattern in the most unique and vibrant way.

CREATIVE COLOUR *in the City*

OPPOSITE AND ABOVE RIGHT **The Emma sofa from George Smith is covered in Susi's beautiful Blue Rose Marbled Velvet. Susi loves mixing modern abstract art with more traditional pieces. Her shell painting and the unknown nude above were framed by Franceschi Cornici in Florence, Italy. Reid Framing made the pair of mirrors from gilded bamboo moulding. The classical head is a gesso copy on a hand-painted plinth made by friends in Florence.**

These days, some of my main sources of inspiration are social media sites such as Instagram and Pinterest, and it was the former that first brought Susi to my attention. I follow so many designers and antiques dealers that I'm always coming across amazing sellers and makers offering the most creative and superbly crafted items. I was immediately captivated by Susi's beautiful collection of wallpapers, fabrics, cushions and lampshades. Her designs are so interesting and original because they're based on her own artworks as well as traditional marbling techniques, which are part of her design DNA after nearly a decade spent living and studying art in Florence.

The influence of those Tuscan years is plain to see, as the former fashion editor's exquisite use of colour is rooted in the rich palette of Renaissance paintings and the frescoes of faded Italian palazzos. Her innovative patterns are all designed to be mixed and matched, and this is demonstrated so effectively within her own home.

I was delighted when Susi agreed that we could include her Bayswater flat in this book – it's such an inspiring example of faded glamour, as well as a wonderful lesson to all in how to combine colour and pattern, and juxtapose old and new. When I first walked in, I gasped, 'Oh my god, it's so beautiful!' I thought the ceilings in our flat were high, but the front of her flat is double-height, which creates an incredible feeling of space.

The flat had been rented out for years, and when Susi decided to make it her pied-à-terre towards the end of 2023, she asked the talented interior designer Pandora Taylor to collaborate with her on the decoration. Together they added the wall panelling to give the space a cosier feel. The lace café curtain hanging at the sitting-room window has a similar effect, breaking up the wide expanse of glass and bringing a soft, feminine touch, making a lovely contrast to the sumptuous full-length linen drapes. I love café curtains and snap up genuine French ones whenever I see them.

ABOVE **I love this little 1960s folding table depicting ballerinas. Susi found it in an antiques shop in Corbridge, Northumberland, along with the Staffordshire dog lamp.**

OPPOSITE AND PAGES 54–55 **Walls in Green Blue by Farrow & Ball, a Christopher Farr rug and curtains in Romo's Launay linen (in lavender and cranberry) set off Susi's designs perfectly. Teal Marbled Velvet is seen on the mid-century chairs and footstool, Multi Plumes Velvet on the cushion and Blue Rose Marbled Velvet on the lampshade. The painting is one of Susi's own pieces depicting the layering of landscape strata from her travels.**

The large, curved living room, where Susi has combined soft greens, blues, mauves, pinks and reds with a mix of her plain, floral and marble-print textiles, is a glamorous space with a hint of 1950s elegance. There are interesting pieces to catch the eye and draw you in, including a gesso copy of a Michelangelo head, a huge rose-print sofa – a recent collaboration between Susi and George Smith – and a seamless assortment of antiques and artworks. When I visit homes like this, I inevitably wish my home was less cluttered – as an avid collector, I have a lot of stuff. I do try to sell, swap or change things around, but some of my treasures are just too precious to part with.

Something I think is so important when decorating a home is the flow from room to room. I'm always aware of the view through a doorway to the space beyond; you've got to consider the flooring and the colours on the walls and ask yourself if they are going to work together. They don't have to match – it's often more interesting when they don't – but they need to entice the eye and not jar with each other. This can often be achieved with a repeated pattern, motif or colour, and Susi has mastered the approach. Looking through to the kitchen from her joyful dining area, with its soft green walls, orange-painted bamboo chairs and red scallop trim framing the rug and doorway, the dusky pink cabinets echo the warm tones of the dining table and the hints of pink in the painting, while the green-and-red-veined quartzite worktop, juxtaposed with a marble-print curtain, mirror the greens, reds and orange.

In Susi's bedroom, the walls and doors are painted an uplifting shade of yellow, setting off the luxurious caramel tones of the bedspread, and the upholstered headboard and cushion in Susi's Yellow Stripy Rose and Saffron Plumes velvets. Not many people put yellow in a bedroom and I love how Susi has mixed it with blue; the effect is so calming. The Yellow Stripy Rose design also features in the en-suite bathroom.

In the hall beyond, the yellow is repeated in the wonderful Dahlia Plumes wallpaper, with the reverse of the door painted in a deep magenta picked out from the design. There are other original touches such as inserting sections of wallpaper into the wall panelling to soften it, which really elevate the effect from the generic. I love going into places and thinking, 'How clever! I never would have thought of that but it really works.' This is definitely one of those homes. It's gorgeous and it makes you smile.

CASE HISTORIES
THE STORY OF ART
KATY HESSEL

ABOVE, RIGHT AND OPPOSITE **Adjacent to the sitting area is the joyful dining space, with an extendable table from Jonathan Adler and a painting by David Denholm. The Cora chairs by Forwood Design have been painted in Bamboozle by Farrow & Ball, with green-striped seat covers by Ian Mankin. I love how the view through to the kitchen is framed by the scalloped border from Ottoline, a motif repeated on the Jennifer Manners rug and Pooky floor lamp. On top of the chinoiserie dresser/hutch sits a copy of a Renaissance head made and painted by a friend in Florence. 'I'm intuitive with colour,' Susi says. 'It's the thread that runs through everything I do.'**

OPPOSITE Designing a small space is always a challenge, but this kitchen is perfect. The green quartzite work surface from Stonecraft London looks so good with the cabinets painted in Light Peachblossom by Little Greene. A curtain in Susi's Dahlia Plumes Linen brings the colours together.

ABOVE LEFT The tumbled-marble tiles from Starel Stones continue into the hall, where Susi added egg-and-dart coving/molding and her Dahlia Plumes wallpaper to make it feel 'like a jewel box'. The bamboo shelving is from Lebove, the mushroom stool in her Aqua Mini Marbled Velvet is from Assieds-Toii and the painting is by Jane Lewis.

ABOVE RIGHT I love how the woodwork/trim and radiator are both painted in Preference Red by Farrow & Ball to complement the wallpaper. The collage by Susi was framed by Franceschi Cornici.

OPPOSITE AND ABOVE **Sudbury Yellow by Farrow & Ball was chosen for the walls in the master bedroom, with the woodwork/trim painted in Dorset Cream. Next to the bathroom door is a series of antique prints of architectural details from Parma in Italy, arranged vertically to make good use of the space.**

RIGHT **The curved chest of drawers/dresser came from Hemswell Antique Centres in Lincolnshire. The mirror's frame, by Franceschi Cornici, was inspired by the façade of the Palazzo dei Diamanti in Ferrara, Italy.**

PAGES 62–63 **The bespoke headboard from R C Dey & Son is upholstered in Susi's Yellow Stripy Rose Velvet and the bedspread is made from her Wheat Veneer Velvet. The cushions are in Aqua Velvet and Saffron Plumes Velvet, while the lampshades are Multi Plumes Linen. The pictures have a pleasing symmetry – above right is a portrait of Susi's mother by her uncle. One of Susi's most treasured possessions is the Yellow Cranes box, which was made out of card by her friend Ann Hepper.**

OPPOSITE AND RIGHT **In the en-suite bathroom, the Yellow Stripy Rose design is repeated as wallpaper. I love the eclectic ornaments that Susi has displayed on the painted shelves, including a French cloisonné jar, china birds and faux coral made from gesso. The marble-topped washstand/vanity and antiqued brass traditional shower fittings are from Victorian Plumbing. The vertical ribs of the fluted shower tiles from Mandarin Stone echo the stripes in the wallpaper, which are in turn echoed in the glass wall light from Pooky. The bamboo-effect mirror is from the same brand.**

"Susi's flat is such an inspiring example of faded glamour, as well as a wonderful lesson to all in how to combine colour and pattern, and juxtapose old and new."

OPPOSITE AND LEFT **Susi's daughter's room has a magical box bed with drawers underneath, painted in Breakfast Room Green and Radicchio by Farrow & Ball. It's such a clever idea for a small space and feels so cocooning and cosy. The Roman blind/shade and the curtain, which screens a hanging space for clothes, are both in Susi's Sage Marbled Velvet. The tiny portrait is by Liorah Tchiprout.**

BELOW LEFT AND RIGHT **The bathroom is a warm and uplifting space in pink, blue and white. The walls are painted in Nancy's Blushes and the washstand/vanity in Stone Blue, both by Farrow & Ball. The wall tiles are from Tiles Direct and the bathroom fittings and mirror cabinet are from Victorian Plumbing. I love the two fans hanging on the wall and the battery-powered lamp from RE in the alcove.**

This townhouse belonging to celebrated British perfumer Azzi Glasser holds a very special place in my heart, as it's the house in Camden, North London that Danny and I owned for four years in the early 2000s, before we sold up and left London for a whole new adventure. It's almost bittersweet to discover that it's still the epitome of faded glamour, but with a twist.

SCENTED *in the City*

OPPOSITE AND ABOVE RIGHT **Azzi had been searching for 10 months for her dream London house with a good-sized garden, when we were introduced by a mutual friend. Azzi arranged a viewing and it was love at first sight. I adore her unique mix of vintage, bespoke and artistic modern pieces, such as the artwork next to the front door by Jake and Dinos Chapman below a South African wall hanging made from tribal headdresses.**

Revisiting this beloved house 20 years after moving away was a strange and nostalgic experience for me. It was the first home that Danny and I bought and renovated together, and we had some great times living here with our young family. It was a huge wrench to leave it in many ways, and initially we thought about renting it out, but then we decided to cut our ties with London. Azzi has been its custodian ever since, layering the interiors with her unique style and personality.

The self-proclaimed 'rebel of the traditional fragrance industry', Azzi is a storyteller at heart – her own brand, launched in 2016, is called The Perfumer's Story by Azzi – and I love the way a home can tell the story of the people who live in it. To me, this is the appeal of period properties, antiques and vintage clothes, too – I have always cherished things with a history. As a teenager, I used to trawl through the rails of vintage clothes at Flip in Covent Garden, a treasure trove of second-hand American denim, lumberjack shirts and army surplus – so cool! My poor mother was horrified at the idea of me bringing home someone else's clothes (she wasn't into vintage, bless her) and would always try to throw them out. I especially love 1920s designs – what a life the flappers led and what fun it seemed! I've collected so many opera coats and beaded dresses from that era over the years and I enjoy thinking about the adventures they must have had. It's a similar thing with antique furniture and objects; these preloved pieces capture my imagination and add so much character to a home.

Much of the downstairs of this house is just as it was when we left – the white-painted floorboards, cornicing/molding, restored by Azzi, the wooden shutters and the open-plan double-height living area where we knocked it through from front to back and took out a ceiling to create a light and airy space with a free-flowing layout. Azzi has painted it in a unifying white, providing a calm backdrop for her eclectic collections.

ABOVE **I used to have a piano in this spot, too! The mix of artworks includes a photograph of Azzi from a shoot by Debbi Clark, two *Teapot* pieces and *Blind Dog* by her son Milo Glasser, *Japanese Bear in Lightbox* by her husband the photographer and artist Dan Glasser and a charcoal work, *Man with Pipe*, by Lorna May Wadsworth. The 1970s blue leather swivel chair is covered with a silk patchwork throw that Azzi found at a vintage market in Morocco.**

These encompass mid-century and vintage furniture and ornaments from around the world, shelves of books, artworks and arrays of scent bottles and candles. It's a live-work space, glamorous with a hint of utilitarianism, and it has a tangible creative energy to it.

The room that Azzi uses as her workspace – and where I've been collaborating with her to create my new range of candles and fragrances – used to be my daughter Daisy's bedroom. The walls are still painted in a gorgeous bespoke colour that my French designer friend Atlantique Ascoli created for me. I wanted a 1920s vibe, and she made up this wonderful paint that's almost a lilac but isn't, as it's also got a lot of grey in it. It's a very tranquil, soothing colour and I love that it's still on the walls.

Azzi's bedroom and adjoining dressing room were once two separate bedrooms, but she cleverly knocked through a wall to make them into one open, light-filled space, which is so cool. When we lived here the floorboards were white, like the downstairs, but Azzi has painted them a sultry dark grey. Her velvet-upholstered antique bed is the focal point of the room, with its delicate lace bedspread and pile of antique cushions. I'm amazed to see that my original lace panel still hangs at the window, filtering the light in a beautiful way.

The main bathroom is very much as it was in our time here: glamorous, feminine and romantic. It's still painted the same pretty shade of dusky pink, grounded by the striking red-and-white chequered tiles, and with another lace panel from my range still hanging at the sash window. I found the roll-top bathtub in a reclamation yard, but Azzi has replaced the gold taps/faucets and filled the shelves on the walls with an abundance of her gorgeous scents and candles. Bathing here must be a sensory delight. I remember being photographed in this bathroom for a property magazine in February 2005, just a few months before we sold the house to Azzi. It really is the most magical home, and we worked and partied hard here. Honestly, I bloody loved it – and if I could, I would buy it from Azzi tomorrow and move back in!

ABOVE **Most of the interior spaces are painted in Farrow & Ball shades of off-white, stone and grey, which create the perfect backdrop for a mix of mid-century, vintage and contemporary pieces, including the black leather sofa and Eames chair. Lighting from the 1950s includes a lamp sourced from Tann Rokka and a glamorous Murano glass chandelier.**

RIGHT The walls of the atelier space are painted in a gorgeous bespoke colour from Ray Munn in Chelsea. I love the mirrored table and the vintage Murano glass chandelier featuring irises and other flowers. The chairs are mid-century designs from Alfies Antique Market in North West London – the green chair is by Robin Day and the leather saddle chairs are by Charlotte Perriand. The giant mirrored glass pyramid containing perfume bottles, *Red Rainstorm*, was designed by Azzi for the Phillips auction house in London's Berkeley Square.

ABOVE Among the objects on the alcove shelves are 1940s scent bottles, a Fig Ambrette candle from The Perfumer's Story by Azzi, a fragrance that she created for perfume house Amaffi and her Lalique crystal award for Best Perfume.

RIGHT In the hearth is a collection of sculptures, figurines and candlesticks, alongside a painting by Laura Cano. The *Bronze Torso* and *Bronze Foot* are by Philippe Mihailovich.

PAGES 74–75 **The sitting-room window overlooks the 42m/140ft-long garden, which is very large by London standards. Planted with grapevines, jasmine, Victorian plum and pear trees, white and black bamboo, palm trees and hydrangeas, it's one of the things Azzi loves most about the house. Star pieces are the Eames chair, the surfboard coffee table and the mocha linen sofa from B&B Italia, with its opulent throw and cushions.**

LEFT **Azzi has repurposed the defunct fireplace to display pieces collected on her travels alongside a vase of flowers. The *Enjoy Yourself* piece hanging over the fireplace is by Helena Bonham Carter.**

ABOVE **On the shelf unit are a few amber ingredient bottles, a Smoked Wood candle from The Perfumer's Story by Azzi and a display of vintage pomanders. I love the confident mix of everyday items and found objects with art and period collections.**

OPPOSITE **Azzi designed the curved shelves in her office, while the green swivel chair is a 1950s piece. Top left on the wall is a record by musician James Lavelle with a gold cover designed by Warren Du Preez and Nick Thornton Jones.**

EAU DE COLOGNE POIVRÉE
COUP DE FOUET CARON
GRACE KELLY

RIGHT **Azzi describes the character of the house as turn-of-the-century French, and nowhere is this influence more apparent than in the master bedroom where the gorgeous 1920s French velvet bed takes centre stage, dressed with a vintage lace throw and antique cushions. Together with the Louis XV gilt chair, 1930s mirror and six-arm chandelier featuring porcelain roses, it's the epitome of faded glamour.**

"I'm amazed to see that my original lace panel still hangs at Azzi's bedroom window, filtering the light in a beautiful way."

ABOVE What used to be another bedroom has been knocked through to make a fabulous dressing room, with rails and hooks offering plenty of hanging room and shelves for shoes and accessories – my idea of absolute heaven where space permits this luxury. The floor has been painted an elegant dark grey, which creates a warmer feel than the white floors downstairs and works beautifully against the mellow taupe walls. The glass-topped wooden table is a pleasing 1950s piece that Azzi found at a vintage shop on Brick Lane in East London.

OPPOSITE I was so happy to discover this pink bathroom virtually unchanged from when we lived here. The roll-top tub was a lucky find at a reclamation yard and I had it re-enamelled and painted gold – so decadent. The picture of the Atlas Mountains in Morocco, propped against the table of perfume bottles, is by Dan.

ABOVE AND RIGHT The shelves are filled with classic perfumes, old scent bottles and Azzi's own fragrances, candles and soaps: Black Moss, Twisted Iris and Fever 54 from The Perfumer's Story by Azzi and Old Books room spray, which she created with Johnny Depp for A Bunch of Stuff. Bathing never smelled so good!

Caledonian Road
ANDY WARHOL
DIARIES
CHATWIN
ARAB ART

The innovative designer Solange Azagury-Partridge is best known for her exceptional jewellery designs and unique interiors. Her beautiful Somerset house was featured in my first book, Faded Glamour, *so I couldn't possibly write a book on city homes without including her treasure trove of a West London flat, as well as both of her extraordinary shops.*

MAVERICK *in the City*

OPPOSITE AND ABOVE RIGHT **Solange finds living with books so life enhancing and would have more if she could: 'It's like having all the worlds and people within them there with you.' Among the mix of art in this sitting room are two nudes by Paul Simonon (left of the left-hand bookcase opposite), another by Polly Borland (above the left-hand bookcase) and a gilt-framed picture by Barry Kamen (above the right-hand bookcase). The Snake Pit rug was designed by Solange.**

Solange and I first met around 20 years ago when she made one of her iconic Written rings for me. She's incredibly creative and I'm a huge fan of her work. Her approach to decorating is unique and very distinctive, mixing styles and eras in an idiosyncratic way. She acquires pieces that she truly loves and the result is a home with real character and authenticity.

I find her interiors so inspiring, especially her bold use of colour. She does things I would not have thought of, such as using an amazing fabric as a wall covering. Her first boutique, which opened in London's Westbourne Grove in 1995, had walls lined in red velvet. Solange never follows trends or plays it safe, and I love an interiors rebel! She's also a fan of pink, my go-to colour for instant warmth. She even created an eponymous paint for her brand, Solange Pink, which is available on request from Papers and Paints in Fulham.

One of the things I adore about this flat is that you can tell it has been lived in for years. Solange is a collector with a great eye, and you don't get this kind of home unless you've given it time to evolve. The mix of furniture, textiles, books and paintings is phenomenal, and she has so many one-off pieces acquired over the years, designed to be custom-made or traded with friends for one of her jewellery pieces. Solange prefers to shop close to home in local boutiques, antiques shops or markets and has often salvaged pieces from the side of the road and given them a new lease of life.

'I don't generally like new things,' she says. 'I love brown furniture, antiques, art bartered with friends. There's no overarching style, but the fact that my eye is the connecting factor between all the pieces gives them a sort of coherence. I like things that look as if they have lived a life, that feel rooted and have some kind of history.'

Solange has lived in this part of West London, near Kensington Gardens, since she was five years old, and she and her husband Murray Partridge have owned this flat for nearly 30 years, so the area feels like home.

ABOVE **Next to the marble fireplace is a chest of drawers/ dresser covered in snake-print Biba fabric. The photo on top is of Solange's mother-in-law in the 1930s; the lemon is by Patrice Moor. Above is a striped painting by Estelle Thompson and a geometric print by Victor Vasarely.**

OPPOSITE **Wedgwood Lilac from Papers and Paints is ideal for this room. The sofa is a 1960s Gio Ponti design and the mid-century dish on the Ochre coffee table is a Vallauris Fat Lava piece. The large painting was swapped with the artist Julia Warr for jewellery and on its right is a work by Reg Gadney. Below it is a chair completely wrapped in pale damask, part of a matching set.**

She recalls walking past the window for years and admiring the intricate cornicing/molding on the ceiling. It was owned by the freeholder of their previous flat a few doors along and he invited them to come and have a look. At the time, each room was divided into individual bedsits that shared one grotty bathroom and an outside loo. But the bones of the place were perfect and the couple were blown away by the black-and-white marble tiles in the entrance hall, as Solange recalls: 'As soon as we walked in and saw that floor, we said, "Oh my god, yes please!".' She and Murray had to put in a kitchen and bathrooms, but other than that they just cleaned it up and painted it. 'The beautiful parquet floor and glorious marble and carved wood fireplaces were all hidden under layers of paint.'

A short walk from the flat, on Chilworth Street, are her studio and two boutiques, Solange and Hotlips by Solange. Each is decorated with her characteristic flair and has a distinct personality, but they all feature vibrant colours, including her custom pink paint, a mix of textures, unusual furniture and decorative details such as hand-painted murals and stained glass.

Walking into the Solange boutique, home to her luxury and bespoke range since 2022, is like stepping into a magical world. The walls are covered in emerald green velvet; stained glass and faceted mirrors glint enticingly as they catch the light; painted forest scenes and lush foliage enchant the eyes; folds of yellow silk damask cover the ceiling. It's like being inside a precious jewellery box.

The Hotlips shop next door is equally stunning but lighthearted, playful and irreverent. The first Hotlips ring, based on the perfect red mouth, was designed in 1998 and was so successful that Solange eventually turned it into a standalone brand in 2018. The shop interior reflects the classic lipstick shades upon which the design was originally based. The aim was to create a colourful, enveloping, private world that allows the client to focus on the jewellery and leave real life behind. What could be more enticing?

FATHERS
AND SONS

LIFE IS

OPPOSITE The same paint colour has been continued into the hall. Looking into the sitting room, the gold sun wall sculpture is by Solange's brother-in-law Roger Partridge and the desk is by Mark Brazier-Jones. Above the door is a skull painting by Billy Childish and on the left is a forest scene by the Japanese artist Yoshihiko Ueda.

RIGHT With its chequered marble floor, the hallway is an inviting space to linger. The green chair is from The World of Differents. Behind the malachite table from Christopher Hodsoll is a chair that Solange found on the street and re-covered in leopard-print velvet. The mirror was left over from when her friend David Collins decorated Marco Pierre White's restaurant Harveys in 1988. The white plaster pieces came from one of Solange's shops.

"Solange's approach is unique and very distinctive, mixing styles and eras in an idiosyncratic way. The result is a home with real character and authenticity."

PAGES 88–89 The mural is a de Gournay wallpaper that Solange couldn't bear to leave behind when she vacated her old Mayfair shop – she reinstalled it here and then the artist Timna Woollard filled in the missing bits. The panelling and cornicing/molding are painted in Pale Wedgwood Blue by Papers and Paints. The sofa was made for Solange's first shop on Westbourne Grove. The little table is 1930s French and the rug is Moroccan.

OPPOSITE One of Solange's favourite rooms is her bedroom, with its chinoiserie-style wallpaper from Watts 1874 and tufted rug by Alexandra Kehayoglou. The rug and the nude painting were bartered for jewellery. The lovely wooden fireplace was revealed beneath layers of paint and brought to life with a neon design by Solange. The chair was a skip/dumpster find reinvigorated with a silver leather seat.

BELOW AND RIGHT I love the mix of designs of these incredible patterned Moroccan tiles on the walls and bathtub panel. The ceiling is painted in Solange Pink, mixed for her by Papers and Paints. The faceted mirror above the sink was made for her shops, while beneath is an oversized bottle of a perfume she created, Stoned. The antique mirror on the windowsill is one of 10 that she bought in Manhattan for clients to try on jewellery.

LEFT At the headquarters of Solange's jewellery business, reclaimed wood panelling lines the meeting-room walls, with the area above painted in Solange Pink and decorated with leaves by the artist Oscar Burnett. Solange designed the Parquet rug and commissioned Bill Amberg to make a gold leather top for the antique table. The shell decoration hanging from the ceiling is from The World of Differents.

ABOVE The building's communal hallway was 'a sad, drab grey', so Solange asked if she could repaint it. The result is a vibrant combination of Solange Pink walls and a lipstick red floor and staircase.

OPPOSITE The studio is also painted in Solange's signature pink, with Persian rugs underfoot. The Chesterfield sofa is from Alfies Antique Market. The photo propped on the antique cabinet is from an ad campaign shot by Katerina Jebb and modelled by Susie Cave. The fringed table is one of Solange's designs. Neon flames enliven the fireplace.

STONED

PAGES 94 AND 95 **The interior of Solange's eponymous boutique is all opulent textures and rich jewel colours. The walls are lined in emerald velvet and the ceiling and woodwork/trim are Solange Pink, with hand-painted foliage and flowers by Oscar Burnett. The painting is by Christian Hidaka. The faceted mirrors, rug and coffee table were all designed by Solange. The sofas were custom-made and the armchair, from George Smith, is covered in one of Solange's kilims.**

ABOVE LEFT AND OPPOSITE **This room is referred to as 'the jungle room' because of the carved wood panels, stained dark brown and painted by Timna Woollard. The windows are made from salvaged stained glass and the ceiling is covered with yellow silk damask. Solange designed the green Hypnotic rug and fringed coffee table, while the sofa was a skip/dumpster find re-covered in leopard print.**

ABOVE RIGHT **In her first shop, Solange had an 'incredibly tatty' early 20th-century desk, which she loved. As the business grew, she created replicas such as this one for her shops all over the world.**

Hotlips

OPPOSITE **The Hotlips by Solange shop next door is decorated in lipstick colours and has a youthful, accessible feel, with its on-brand neon in the fireplace. The woodwork/trim is painted in Solange Pink, set off by a scarlet rug, and the walls are covered in a dreamy cloudscape by Fine & Dandy Co. The mirror is based on the faceted ones made for the Solange boutique but in the shape of a mouth.**

LEFT **Solange designed the stained-glass window. The sofa is a three-seater version of the smaller ones next door, here covered in red leather.**

ABOVE **The ceiling is hand-painted in pink and red stripes to resemble a circus tent. 'I wanted this shop to feel happy and exciting and jolly,' Solange explains. Hanging from the centre is a giant red gift bow made from canvas-backed plastic.**

I have known this amazing five-storey Edwardian townhouse for many years because it used to belong to a friend, the talented designer Sera Hersham-Loftus, who affectionately named it Chocolate Towers due to its brown exterior. For the past 15 years it has been the London family home of Austrian entrepreneur Carmen Haid, the founder of Atelier Mayer, which sells rare vintage objects and luxury lifestyle products.

SOUK STYLE *in the City*

OPPOSITE **In the hallway, burgundy walls and a reclaimed parquet floor set a dramatic tone. Bullion-fringed lights inspired by Beirut's Hotel Albergo and an ornate gilt mirror bring glamour to the space.**

ABOVE RIGHT **Carmen believes that 'an eclectic mix gives each room its soul'. Here, an antique table is juxtaposed with layers of Peruvian carpet cushions and embroidered textiles featuring Central Asian Suzani motifs.**

Carmen and I share a deep appreciation for antiques, fine craftsmanship and vintage pieces that are steeped in history. She sources all the pieces she sells herself, from vintage dealers, auctions, flea markets and on her travels, and commissions local artisans to create bespoke items for clients around the world. Carmen's business is based in Marrakesh and Paris as well as London, and the influence of those vibrant cities, along with her Austrian heritage, is evident throughout her home. The interior has a distinctly global feel, offering a slightly more bohemian interpretation of faded glamour. It's intriguing, stunning and just a little bit different.

Stepping inside is like entering a serene oasis in the heart of the city. The house is a wonderful mix of light-filled living spaces and cosy seating areas anchored on elaborately patterned Persian rugs that add opulence. Everywhere you look there are interesting pieces of furniture, many of them featuring intricate carving or upholstered in sumptuous jewel-coloured textiles and scattered with an array of embroidered, woven, printed and trimmed cushions. The walls are filled with artworks, and there are so many unusual lights, mirrors and artefacts that it truly is a feast for the eyes. Cut flowers and leafy plants contribute to the exotic atmosphere. I am always envious of people whose homes are full of lush greenery, as I have a knack for killing plants. Friends often gift them to me, insisting, 'You can't possibly kill this one.' Yet a few months later, without fail, it's dead.

Different eras and cultures have come together to give each room its own personality. There is somewhere to suit every mood or activity. Business meetings are held in the panelled Secessionist *fumoir*, which opens onto the prettiest of courtyard gardens. Then there are meals with family and friends in the airy Gustav Klimt-inspired kitchen-dining space. Carmen also enjoys curling up with a good book in 'the tent room' or relaxing in the drawing room for drinks at the end of the day.

Upstairs feels like stepping into a riad. The original flooring is a mix of white-painted floorboards and matt dark-stained parquet, again covered with the most gorgeous patterned rugs. I appreciate the authenticity of old wooden floors, but in bedrooms and bathrooms the warmth and softness of rugs under bare feet is more than welcome. On the walls, there are expanses of white-painted exposed brickwork, which has so much more character than smooth plaster and gives a simple, rustic feel. Carmen has used beautifully crafted cutwork wooden screens and panels as doors and room dividers – such a clever way of bringing pattern and texture into a space.

The master bedroom encompasses a tranquil dressing area at one end and the most stunning bathroom with a walk-in shower and freestanding roll-top bathtub at the other. Being right at the top of the house, it has amazing views and incredible light. The Japanese-style wooden bed is low to the floor and is topped with a glorious multicoloured patchwork bedspread. Like me, Carmen has a cupboard full to the brim with the most exquisite vintage bedspreads, though hers are Oriental and mine are mostly French or English. I love having different bed coverings to choose from as an effortless way to change the look, depending on the season or your mood.

In the en-suite, more carved panels screen off the shower area, where the limestone walls and sloping ceiling have been lined with Turkish hand-painted decorative tiles with a green and blue botanical design. The beams in the bathroom have been painted deep emerald, echoing the green in the tiles.

Carmen maintains that it's still early days with this house and she hasn't quite finished it yet, but I wonder how many homes ever feel truly finished, especially when their owner is constantly coming across the most covetable pieces all in a day's work. That's certainly the case for me, and in my view some of the most interesting homes are those that are constantly evolving – it keeps things fresh and exciting!

OPPOSITE **The panelled walls of the *fumoir*, in crisp white and navy detailing, were inspired by the Wiener Werkstätte style of Austrian architect Josef Hoffmann. A vintage shirt cabinet, repainted and repurposed as a toy cupboard, stands alongside a pair of petrol velvet Jean-Michel Frank armchairs. Atelier Mayer aubergine velvet drapes dress the window.**

RIGHT **Inspired by the art of Gustav Klimt, the glamorous kitchen features classic white metro tiles and a striking brass chandelier by Koloman Moser with fluted glass shades. Josef Hoffmann dining chairs surround the table, which is covered with a Summerill & Bishop tablecloth and vases of cut flowers.**

LEFT **This intimate and inviting end of the living room is framed by a tent made from vintage Turkish Suzani textiles with hand-painted poles. The wooden shutters, dark floorboards and carved seating are softened by the mix of textiles, antique books, bespoke fringed lamp and Persian heirloom rug. A Carlo Bugatti inlaid wall piece adds to the room's global character.**

OPPOSITE **Deep-pile velvets are used for upholstery throughout the house. I especially love this burgundy armchair with the Persian rug and periwinkle blue walls. A painting of roses by Sir Matthew Smith hangs alongside an 1887 Orientalist work by Emmanuel de Dieudonné entitled *A Turkish Beauty with a Narguilé*.**

"Carmen's business is based in Marrakesh and Paris as well as London, and the influence of those vibrant cities, along with her Austrian heritage, is evident throughout her home."

ABOVE The spacious double reception room has been decorated and furnished as two distinct yet harmonious living spaces. Above the arched opening is a screen that pulls down to transform the tented area into a home cinema. On either side, the pair of traditional radiators and the painting by British-Brazilian artist Olivier Mourão, opposite the one by Emmanuel de Dieudonné, create balance and drama.

RIGHT In this tranquil light-filled space, the custom-made blue sofa is framed by the grand bay window. The vintage tables echo the wooden shutters, while an abundance of greenery reinforces the connection with the garden. A mirrored disco ball overhead adds a touch of unexpected charm.

OPPOSITE **Olivier Mourão's vivid painting *Carmen and the Vase* crowns the fireplace with theatrical flair, alongside a surreal composition by the English painter Ivan Seal and an opulent carved throne chair by Carlo Bugatti.**

ABOVE **This rare Carlo Bugatti wall hanging and throne chair belonged to the art dealer Martin Summers when he lived in his legendary home in London's Chelsea, made in the mid 1970s by knocking through a row of artists' studios.**

RIGHT **The sculptural staircase, designed by American artist Danny Lane, has hand-forged iron balustrades with fluid scrollwork and lattice detailing. The doors to Carmen's office are painted in Majorelle blue, a vibrant shade associated with the garden of the same name in Marrakesh, with a frosted-glass circular window. The fringed velvet wall lights were inspired by ones in the Hôtel Bourg Tibourg in Paris.**

LEFT A stunning Chadder & Co. bathtub sits on the original flooring painted in a geometric pattern. The hand-painted bathroom door and cupboards provide texture and detail.

OPPOSITE The dreamlike figurative collage by Olivier Mourão brings softness and elegance to this bedroom, while a richly embroidered bedspread and vibrant rug add texture and warmth. Whitewashed brick walls keep the space calm.

PAGE 112 This Moorish-inspired bathroom has hand-painted Ottoman Iznik tiles and carved wooden panels, with a Mughal latticework design around the shower. The green-painted rafters tie in with the roll-top tub and natural greenery.

PAGE 113 In the attic bedroom, a surrealist landscape by Edward Burra hangs above a Japanese platform bed draped in a jewel-toned silk patchwork bedspread with Banjara-style embroidery.

PAGES 114–115 This attic retreat is filled with natural light by day, then at night vintage Murano glass lights and Moroccan lanterns provide atmospheric lighting. Built-in cupboards line one wall, opposite the tiled fireplace and a collection of framed tropical butterflies.

DISFARMER

This beautiful home in New York City's West Village belongs to the Danish-Peruvian supermodel and photographer Helena Christensen. Her charming, comfortable and stylish apartment is filled with antiques, books, artworks and mementoes collected over many years. It is hard to believe that this enchanting oasis is in the heart of Manhattan.

HIDEAWAY *in the City*

OPPOSITE **In this living room, Stone Blue by Farrow & Ball is a timeless backdrop for the eclectic mix of furniture, pictures, ceramics and books. The elegant antique sofa and armchair are from John Derian and the Nawabari velvet ottoman is from BoConcept, the Danish brand for which Helena is the global artistic director. The floral paintings are all local antique finds, while the wonderful shell cushion is from Tamar Mogendorff.**

ABOVE RIGHT **Helena's Australian Shepherd dog Kuma loves to get cosy on the sheepskin rug.**

I first met Helena through our mutual friend, the actress Liv Tyler. I remember being quite blown away, not only by her beauty and the incredible dress she was wearing, but also by her wicked sense of humour. We instantly hit it off and bonded over interiors and style.

Even though Helena and I live in different countries, we've kept in touch, and I love seeing her Instagram stories of her beautiful homes, which are all so inspiring – this apartment in Manhattan, her clapboard country retreat in the Catskills in upstate New York, her bolthole in Copenhagen and her summer beach house on the coast of Denmark. The latter was featured in my previous book, *Faded Glamour by the Sea*, so I was thrilled that she agreed to let me include her West Village apartment in this book.

Helena has such effortless style and a knack for hunting out the most gorgeous antiques and vintage pieces. She's a fellow maximalist who can't resist a treasure that has a past and a story to tell, and she has such a talent for creating rooms with a lived-in, cosy and super-stylish aesthetic. She is not afraid of colour, but always chooses a palette that promotes a feeling of tranquillity and doesn't compete with all the quirky objects and artworks on display. She also loves plants and books, which bring a natural softness and warmth to a space, as well as a relaxed intellectual vibe. I recently visited Charleston near Lewes, East Sussex, the home of Vanessa Bell, Duncan Grant and other key members of the Bloomsbury Group during the interwar years, and this apartment is somehow reminiscent of that bohemian artists' house, especially in the use of colour.

Helena bought this property, a former paper factory built in 1856, in 2000 from the American artist Jim Dine, who used it as his studio. 'I loved that it belonged to a painter I very much admired,' she says. The other aspects that appealed to her were its high ceilings, big windows and French doors leading outside to a peaceful plant-filled sanctuary.

LUCIAN FREUD
LUCIAN FREUD
John Galliano
MARTINE SITBON — Alternative Vision

LEFT **Rustic-industrial style meets old-school glamour: a Staerk Collection rug softens the original floorboards, while antiques, pictures, plants and books are juxtaposed with the exposed brick wall. The vintage plan chest is home to Helena's photography prints and above it is a painting by local artist Austin Eddy. The lifebuoy on the wall is a prop from the movie *Cape Fear* – it was a gift from Rocco Laspata and Charles DeCaro, creative directors of the luxury-brand advertising agency Laspata DeCaro. Helena likes to keep the doors to the garden open during the summer so she can enjoy the birdsong.**

ABOVE **Oil paintings, photographs, prints, drawings and even pages from antique books are hung and propped up all over the apartment. The little figures were made by an artist in Kenya using pieces of wood and found objects.**

OPPOSITE **Helena is a self-confessed bibliophile and the shelves in the study area are crammed with stacks of books on art, photography and nature, as well as poetry and novels. The big windows are not overlooked, so Helena has kept them curtain-free to maximize the light.**

'The terrace is very special. It's full of plants, trees and flowers, and in the summertime there are nests with baby doves and blackbirds, and butterflies flutter around.' There are also two working fireplaces, for which she is hugely grateful in the winter months: 'They make the apartment so cosy.'

As an artist's studio, it was just one big space with no separate rooms, a small loo and barely any kitchen area. Helena created an open-plan kitchen and dining space, plus a main bedroom, two guest rooms, a luxurious bathroom and a guest cloakroom. The ceiling height also made it possible for her to put in a spiral staircase leading up to a small loft.

The kitchen and dining area benefit from the most beautiful light in the morning, while the main living room, which has floor-to-ceiling doors that open onto the leafy courtyard garden, is warmed up by the afternoon sun and bathed in a magical glow until sunset. In a city where so many apartments are very contemporary and polished, I love how Helena has retained elements of the industrial past, such as the rustic exposed brickwork, but softened it with homely, pretty details, resulting in a space that is at once incredibly cool and very welcoming.

I admire everything about this wonderful apartment, which has something intriguing in every corner and really epitomizes the faded glamour look – honestly, I could happily move in tomorrow! As with all the best homes, you can tell it has been decorated and furnished with objects collected and curated over time, by someone with a real eye. Helena has a passion for trawling antiques shops and flea markets, and New York City and its nearby towns have proved to be rich hunting grounds – the majority of the items here were found locally.

She tells me, 'I wanted the space to feel like an old country house in Tuscany – serene and peaceful, full of art and colours, with couches and armchairs to fall into with a book. I love living in NYC because it's so alive, electric and intense, but I appreciate coming home to this calm, beautiful nest, where I can hear birds sing on the terrace all day long.'

PLANT
THE BEST OF
ARAKI
RANKIN
Diane Arbus

PLANT
RUNNING HEAD

OPPOSITE The beautiful leather-topped writing desk is from O'Sullivan Antiques in Dublin, which belongs to Helena's friend Chantal O'Sullivan. The chairs were found closer to home at the 26th Street Flea Market in NYC. Helena bought the hand-painted canvas wall hanging from a little gallery in the 6th arrondissement when she was living in Paris.

PAGE 124 Hanging above the fireplace is a print of *Predator* by the street artist Gaia. On the mantelpiece are lots of curious objects, along with the painting *Autumnal Gods* by Michael McGrath. Helena is a UNHCR Goodwill Ambassador and the artisan candles are from Made51, the agency's initiative supporting refugee craftsmanship. A couple of pictures are casually affixed to the fire surround with washi tape, including a page from a book depicting *The Hobo* by American painter John Currin.

PAGE 125 In this seating area, the grey-painted floorboards have been finished with a shiny varnish. The glamorous sofa is from Ellison Studios. Around it are fabulous vintage finds including the mirror, flower painting and Hollywood Regency side table. I feel especially drawn to the cute cabinet filled with glassware.

ABOVE I love creating a gallery wall by putting a variety of pictures together – florals, portraits and nudes, for example – to make it a little unexpected. This collection of black-and-white photographs and drawings includes some of Helena's own pictures and her son Mingus's childhood artworks.

TOM BARIL
DIANE ARBUS REVELATIONS

LEFT **The kitchen area has a real 1950s vibe – I love how the Smeg dishwasher adds an unexpected pop of red in between the glossy cream cabinets. On the open shelves is a colourful array of assorted pottery and vintage kitchen paraphernalia, while hanging below is a seascape from an antique market alongside *Two-Way Inn* by Jordan Sullivan and the 2020 Forever Stamps collection celebrating the work of Ruth Asawa.**

OPPOSITE **This amazing industrial black chest of drawers/dresser was found by Helena in an antique store. Every drawer is full – one with concert tickets, others with cards and letters, jewellery, make-up photographs and 665 Polaroid film. From left to right, the artworks include a large horse painting by a Canadian artist, a numbered print of Lucian Freud's portrait of John Minton, a black-and-white flower print by Hugo Guinness and a painting of two women by Deng Shiqing.**

BJÖRK
VESPERTIN
NEW ALBUM AUGUST 28

OPPOSITE **Helena bought the piano a long time ago from the American rapper and record producer Q-Tip. She used to play a lot when she was a child, 'but now I just sit down once in a while and play a little Chopin,' she admits. The papier-mâché woman dragging a dress behind her is by Helena's friend, the artist Lisbeth McCoy, who passed away in 2024: 'She was very gifted and I love that serene piece of art. I light a candle by it every evening.' The cut-out page is a portrait of Helena by Francesco Clemente for *Vogue Italia*, and the large Victorian oil painting is from an antiques market.**

RIGHT **The picture of the dog-looking man is Helena's favourite piece of art, painted by Mingus when he was seven years old. The other works are from local antique stores and the old sleigh decorated with planes came from upstate New York. The two painted bottles were a lucky find in a Housing Works thrift shop.**

OPPOSITE **The tranquil bedroom is painted in Belvedere Blue by Farrow & Ball. The bed was bought from ABC Carpet & Home about 30 years ago and was originally a four-poster that Helena adapted to fit the room. It's dressed with a beautiful antique patchwork quilt and a teddy bear from The Dandy, Sunny Ruffalo's upstate store that has sadly closed. The bedside tables/nightstands and hand-painted lamps are from a local antiques market, as are the dark and detailed nude and floral paintings, which probably date from the 19th century.**

ABOVE **This pretty urban garden, filled with vines and flowering hydrangeas, is remarkably green and secluded for an outside space in the centre of New York City. One thing I really miss during the summer at our flat in London is a terrace to sit out on, with a table and chairs surrounded by leafy plants and flowers.**

"Helena has such effortless style and a knack for hunting out gorgeous antiques and vintage pieces. She's a fellow maximalist who can't resist a treasure that has a past and a story to tell."

This unique London property is not a private home, but the working studio and creative hub of an innovative portrait painter who is one of Britain's most prominent contemporary artists. In 2017 Vanity Fair *declared, 'in 21st-century Britain you do not exist as a public figure unless you have been painted by Jonathan Yeo.'*

STUDIO *in the City*

OPPOSITE **The garden room has a mid-century feel with its ochre walls, floor-to-ceiling curtains and geometric rug. A pair of vintage green velvet sofas offers an inviting space for conversation. The sconces are 1950s Swedish glass and brass, while the chandeliers are from Soho Home.**

ABOVE RIGHT **The artworks in this room include (clockwise from top left): *Nicole Kidman*, *John Cooper Clarke*, *Stephen Fry* and *Rhytidectomy I*, all by Jonathan Yeo.**

Jonathan, also known as Jonny, has worked with countless celebrated subjects, from A-list actors to political leaders. Spectacularly, in May 2024 he unveiled his highly publicised 'red' portrait of King Charles, the first official likeness since the coronation. On the opposite side of the spectrum, as a favour to a friend, Jonny helped Danny out by designing one of his solo album covers.

I've known Jonny and his wife Shebah Ronay for many years – we once found ourselves staying in the same hotel in Miami for Christmas and, although it was totally unplanned, our two families had such a fun time together. Not only is Jonny an unbelievably talented artist, he's also a really cool guy with a passion for designing interiors and a great eye for sourcing furniture and putting it all together.

I really wanted to include his studio in the book, as for me it illustrates how a formerly industrial building can have new life breathed into it when it falls into the right hands. It has been transformed into a creative space that exudes faded glamour in an understated way. All cities are shaped by their industrial past, from the wool and cloth trade of Frome, my home town in Somerset, to the development of the docks and associated industries in the East End of London, where my father grew up. A book on *Faded Glamour in the City* didn't feel complete without a nod to the industrial history of this vibrant metropolis.

In 2021, Jonny had to move out of the set of studios that he'd used for a decade and he spent months searching across London for an interesting space. When he was shown this building, which had been constructed as a factory for pianos and organs in the late 19th century, he loved it at first sight: 'The unique triangular shape, the double-height atrium, its relatively hidden location at the end of a road, the original steel-framed windows overlooking a beautiful park, the Victorian industrial features, its great light and overall sense of calm all added to its allure.'

ABOVE ***Planten & Blomen*** **by Jonathan Yeo, a limited-edition archival pigment print, hangs on the wall behind the sofa and elegant mid-century glass and brass coffee table. The little striped suitcase used for storage and the lush plants add to the homey feel.**

OPPOSITE **The focal point of the meeting area is the 1960s rosewood and metal Arkana Tulip table by Maurice Burke, surrounded by vintage leather chairs. Behind it, the Ladderax shelving unit is filled with colour-coordinated books. Propped up on the lowest shelf is Jonny's portrait of Taron Egerton as Elton John in the film *Rocketman*.**

Previously the offices of a music production company, the interior was tired, functional and dated when Jonny took ownership, so he spent 10 months renovating it, meaning he had no proper space to paint for nearly a year. He removed the main staircase and installed new spiral steps of his own design, and replaced some internal walls and doors with steel-framed ones, echoing the windows. When the floorboards in the painting studio upstairs were taken up, the original ones were revealed, complete with patches of old paint and lacquer that may date back to the building's early use.

I remember Jonny's excitement when he bought this place and the first time I saw it I could see why. The light streaming in is incredible, like a warm glow, and he's decorated and furnished it so beautifully that it feels like a home. My first words were, 'Wow, it's so cool, I could live here!'

Jonny's aim was to create a series of separate yet connected workspaces for different studio practices, whether painting, sculpting, working on tech projects or hosting meetings. The amazing 7m/23ft-high atrium at the centre is the main social and meeting area – it's also been the setting for some great drinks parties!

The main influence on the design of the interior was the building itself, as Jonny wanted to reference its unique history but bring it up to date. He has incorporated plants and wooden furniture to soften the industrial feel. 'It's a mix of contemporary and mid-century design interspersed with vintage curios and oddities that I've collected over the years. I've integrated some furniture from the 1950s and gradually added newer pieces.'

Some of Jonny's favourite places to source furniture are Ed Butcher, The Old Cinema, Alfies Antique Market and Kempton antiques market. He also picked up some pieces online. 'Vintage shopping is quite addictive and I'm often found at the local flea market when I travel to other countries – Istanbul and Paris are particular favourites,' he confessed. A man after my own heart!

THE ART OF REBELLION
SOTTSASS
Basquiat
Aesthetic Surgery
JOHN CURRIN
WALTER SICKERT
Manet
POP ART
Weston

OPPOSITE Jonny replaced the original staircase with this bespoke spiral, designed by him and Yeo Studio. Hand-painted in matt black with brass inlays, it was manufactured and installed by Metalworks London. Nearby is a vintage barber's chair, a neon light from Gods Own Junkyard in Walthamstow and *Sienna (Pregnant)* by Jonathan Yeo.

ABOVE Beneath the sculptural stairs is another meeting space furnished with a vintage dining table, leather chairs and rosewood sideboard. A vintage easel displays *Paradox of Progress Trials* by Jonathan Yeo; another two works from this series are propped up against the wall. Hanging behind the table on the left is *Lily Cole as Helen of Troy* and on the right is *Cara I (Goggles)*.

RIGHT In between piles of books is *Maquette for Homage to Paolozzi (Self Portrait)* by Jonathan Yeo, created using virtual reality technology – the full-size bronze piece is shown on pages 138–139.

500 PORTRAITS
Saul Bass
Philip Guston
MICHAEL BORREMANS
Breakfast with Lucian
Georges Braque
KIPPENBERGER
TASCHEN
JONATHAN YEO
IN THE FLESH
MAGRITTE
ADRIAN GHENIE
Contemporary Art in Print

PAGES 138–139 AND LEFT **The main atrium is the beating heart of this fabulous studio. It's a fabulous lofty space where Jonny hosts gatherings and drinks parties, but it feels like the most glamorous mid-century home with the vintage sideboard, bespoke cabinetry by LT Carpentry and a 1960s Stilnovo chandelier. I always love the edgy mood that animal print brings to a room and this zebra velour 1970s Howard Keith Diplomat sofa is a star piece. Alongside it is a pair of Rolland armchairs and a Carter coffee table in Rosso Levanto marble, both from Soho Home. On the wall behind are *The Unteleported Man* and *The Simulacra* by Jonathan Yeo.**

OPPOSITE **A pair of cognac leather Bruno Mathsson Jetson lounger chairs draws the eye towards the yellow office with its vintage Ladderax shelving unit and reclaimed wall light. Jonny explains, 'I wanted to create a sense that there's always more to explore. No matter where you are in the building, you're teased by glimpses of the other spaces through semi-transparent curtains, foliage or fluted glass.'**

SUPER
GILBERT & GEORGE
ANDY

PAGES 142–143 **The building's triangular shape is evident in the main studio. Vintage gym stools are the perfect height for resting palettes on, alongside easels from Mabef and R Baldwin of Chelsea. Finished works in this room include *Giancarlo Esposito, Sophia Loren, Sir Peter Blake, Maxine Peake, Pierce Brosnan* and *Paradox of Progress Trial*.**

ABOVE **This study for the portrait of King Charles that was unveiled in May 2024 was part of the four-year process, which involved four-hour-long sittings at Highgrove and Clarence House. Jonny loves to study his subjects in depth and capture the many sides of their character.**

OPPOSITE **A 2014 portrait of actress Maxine Peake in the painting studio. 'Part of my work has always involved people coming to sit for portraits, so it is important to have an environment that is as interesting and welcoming to visitors as it is conducive to creative working for me and my small team,' Jonny explains.**

"I really wanted to include Jonny's studio in the book, as for me it illustrates how a formerly industrial building can have new life breathed into it when it falls into the right hands."

MA JIAN
TWENTIETH CENTURY POSTERS
GILBERT & GEORGE
GILBERT & GEORGE
EL PRADO
The English Face
GAUGUIN
GLENN BROWN

ABOVE **There are several interconnecting spaces across the two upstairs floors that Jonny and his team use for different aspects of the creative process. This painting studio is furnished with mid-century pieces, including a 1970s black leather Ekornes Stressless chair, a vintage glass cabinet and a traditional plan chest.**

OPPOSITE **Much like me, Jonny can't resist a vintage find, so his paintings are interspersed with unusual pieces and curious trinkets including (clockwise from top left): a vintage dressmaker's mannequin wearing a gas mask; *Sophia Loren* behind jars and pots of paintbrushes; a neon hotel sign above a painting of Jonny's daughter Tabitha and, on the plan chest among stacks of books, a vintage wooden artist's mannequin and *Helena Bonham Carter (Study)*.**

PAGE 148 **The snug, a small annex off the main painting studio, is Jonny's favourite space in the building. It has two large windows that look out over the trees in the park, which inspired Jonny to clad the walls in reclaimed wood and add lots of greenery. The mid-century Case Forum sofa was designed by Robin Day.**

PAGE 149 **The director's office is furnished with a vintage Johannes Andersen coffee table, an old leather sofa and stacking chairs by Giancarlo Piretti for Castelli. *Mappa Dell'Antico Futuro (Study)* by Jonathan Yeo is displayed on the easel next to the vintage desk and Eames desk chair.**

Jonathan Yeo

MASTERPIECES OF THE BRITISH MUSEUM
SOHO SOCIETY
THINGS COME APART

HOTEL

RETHINKING CONSCIOUSNESS
VAN GOGH to PICASSO
Cézanne
Tate
GREAT FRENCH PAINTINGS
THE BARNES FOUNDATION
JENNY SAVILLE

VENEZIA

This stunning five-storey townhouse in North West London certainly has the wow factor. As well as being the family home of stylish and talented designer Lara Bohinc MBE, it doubles as the showroom for her collections of award-winning furniture and objects. As such, it exemplifies the perfect marriage of period features and modern design.

MODERN GLAMOUR *in the City*

ABOVE RIGHT **Lara has widened some of the doorways to open up the interiors. Her bold use of colour throughout gives the period property a modern edge. The hallway's bespoke petrol blue walls provide a tonal backdrop for art from Norbert Schoerner's series *Bondage Bonsai*. Lara's red Saturn chair for Bohinc Studio adds a pop of red.**

OPPOSITE **The concrete floor and grey-painted brickwork lend an industrial feel to this room, which is furnished with pieces by Lara for Bohinc Studio: the Kissing sofa and Big Girl armchair in red bouclé, Saturn pouffe and Schatzi armchair in cream bouclé, Planetaria brass floor lamp, Macaroon ash-wood table and Bubu porcelain vase.**

Before Lara bought this early Victorian house in 2019, she had been searching for a while for a period property that hadn't been knocked about too much, and with all the wonderful features and proportions that make those houses so beautiful still intact. This house hadn't been touched for around 40 years and required extensive structural work, including the enlarging of the doorways to enhance the sense of space, new plumbing and electrics and the restoration of many of the original decorative details such as the cornicing/molding and fireplaces. However, it had the authenticity that Lara was looking for, along with high ceilings and large sash windows that ensure the rooms are filled with natural light.

Lara's clever and sometimes unexpected use of materials, colour and texture has made the house feel sophisticated and modern without destroying the integrity of the building. The exposed brick walls and raw concrete floors, more often seen in warehouses and industrial-style interiors than in Victorian properties, bring a very cool edge. Perhaps the thing I love most about this house is the way it illustrates how a clever contrasting of eras and styles can highlight and enhance the beauty of each in a unique and impactful way.

Lara studied industrial design at the Ljubljana Academy of Fine Arts and Design in Slovenia, where she grew up, before moving to London to complete an MA in metalwork at the Royal College of Art. She then spent a decade designing jewellery for Cartier before founding her own design studio in 2016, to focus on creating functional pieces for living – furniture, lighting and objects – using a variety of natural and sustainable materials. Prioritizing traditional craft techniques and artisanal expertise in conjunction with high-tech innovations, the studio produces its own collections alongside public and private commissions, as well as selective collaborations with companies such as Roll & Hill, Phelippeau Tapissier, Serafini and Kasthall.

PAGES 152–153 AND LEFT **The period townhouses in this part of London have huge sash windows, and these ones have the original wooden shutters, too. Lara has cleverly made a feature of the windows by painting the entire area around them, including the cornicing/molding above, in Blush by Little Greene.**

OPPOSITE **The same palette is carried through into the kitchen. The marble and brass Lunar dining table is the focal point, topped with a Jupiter vase and surrounded by Trevor chairs, all by Lara for Bohinc Studio. The Moonrise chandelier is a collaboration between Lara and Roll & Hill.**

In addition to being a home to Lara, her husband and teenage daughter, the interior was conceived to showcase the studio's designs in a residential setting that would complement the brand's aesthetics. Lara's designs are bold, sculptural and sensuous statement pieces that are strikingly juxtaposed with the exposed brick walls, painted in shades of earthy brown, terracotta, plaster pink and dusky grey, and the concrete and parquet floors. I was struck by her bold use of colour. The tones that she has put together work in such an unexpected way – the pops of cherry red, cerulean blue and graphic black and white against the more subtle hues. It's a palette I never would have thought of, but it looks fantastic. I particularly love how she has painted the fire surrounds in the same colour as the walls, but the window frames, shutters and cornicing/molding above the windows in a contrasting tone. It's such a clever way to bring a contemporary feel to a room with period features.

Across its five floors, the house has the feeling of a collection of vignettes with different areas having different moods and atmospheres yet creating a seamless flow. Repeated shapes, materials and colours all reinforce the connection between the spaces. Every one is amazing, but I have to confess that I absolutely adore the main bedroom and its adjacent bathroom, which is also Lara's favourite space. The light-filled bedroom, with its zigzag wooden floor and pink-painted brick walls, overlooks her lush leafy garden below. Behind the bed, in place of a traditional headboard, is Lara's East of the Moon rug for Kasthall in rich shades of rust tempered with grey. What a brilliant idea! Its geometric shapes are echoed in the Celeste console and Saturn pouffe, and were also the inspiration for the incredible custom-made shower clad with offcuts of marble from the Italian marble specialists Serafini. Just imagine taking a bath in this bathroom – it's the height of glamour!

Somehow Lara has managed to create both a superbly curated showpiece of a house and a warm and comfortable family home that is filled with light and creative energy. I really loved spending time in this house; it's a very special place.

LEFT In the office space, the Blush paint has been extended from the window frame down onto the concrete floor, cleverly creating a zone for the Kipferl desk in rosa portugalo marble and the cream bouclé Afternoon chair. Both pieces, along with the brass Ion table light on the mantelpiece, are by Lara for Bohinc Studio. The huge leafy plants on either side of the window add natural texture and colour.

ABOVE I love how Lara puts together different pieces from all her collections to create distinct seating areas. In the other corner of this room is a marble Profiterole table, Trevor dining chair and brass Ion floor light, all by Lara for Bohinc Studio.

ABOVE LEFT **In this sitting area, the organic form of the Willow light that Lara designed for Gallery FUMI was inspired by an ancient Japanese garden. Made of oxidized blackened brass, it has an Art Deco feel, as does the bronzed ceramic Fortress Column vase by Bohinc Studio.**

ABOVE RIGHT **The exposed brick walls and woodwork/trim are painted in rich Baked Cherry, slightly lighter Tuscan Red and dark grey Lamp Black, all by Little Greene. The Camaleonda sofa is vintage B&B Italia. Behind it is the South Pole wall hanging from Lara's collaboration with Kasthall called From the Sun to the Moon.**

OPPOSITE **The revolving coffee table, designed in 1969 by the Italian photographer Willy Rizzo, sits on an East of the Moon rug by Lara for Kasthall. The black-and-white armchair is another vintage find.**

"Lara's clever and sometimes unexpected use of materials, colour and texture has made the house feel sophisticated and modern without destroying its integrity."

LEFT **Parquet flooring laid in a large-scale chevron design creates a striking geometric pattern underfoot. It is a foil for the curvaceous Derriere chair and Peaches pouffe, both designed by Lara for Bohinc Studio in celebration of the female form.**

OPPOSITE **Lara has placed her lacquered Ribbon desk and the chairs designed by Maarten Baas for Lensvelt at an unexpected angle near the floor-to-ceiling window, creating a dynamic flow of energy. On the wall behind is a brushed brass Moonrise sconce from Lara's collaboration with Roll & Hill and on the desk is a Collision table light and a red Fortress Tower vase, both by Lara for Bohinc Studio. The same vase in blue stands on one of two white ash Profiterole side tables, which are highlighted against the dark grey wall. On the taller one is a vintage brass table lamp.**

SKETCH

OPPOSITE LEFT **In the master bedroom, the walls and woodwork/trim are painted in Blush by Little Greene, which tones with the parquet floor. The elegant Celeste console in a brass and burnt black finish is such a glamorous piece alongside the Saturn pouffe, both Lara's designs for Bohinc Studio.**

OPPOSITE ABOVE RIGHT **Another Profiterole coffee table, this time in nero marquina marble, sits in a corner of the room with a bronze Fortress Tower vase of flowers in toning colours.**

OPPOSITE BELOW RIGHT **In an adjoining room, Lara's Celeste chair in bronze, brass and cream wool becomes almost a sculpture, highlighted against the dramatic wall painted in Lamp Black by Little Greene.**

ABOVE **An East of the Moon rug in rust, designed by Lara for Kasthall, hangs on the wall behind the bed. Inspired by a Zen garden, it softens the brick wall and adds textural interest. The To the Moon cushions in rose are from the same collection. The archway leading to the bathroom features built-in wardrobes/closets in black ash. Beside the bed is a Planetaria table light.**

RIGHT A pair of surface-mounted basins in the master bathroom have been built into a custom-made ribbed cabinet in black ash with brass legs and trim. The wall is clad in marble in one of Lara's signature geometric designs, a collaboration with Serafini. The parquet flooring in the bathroom is laid in the same chevron design as elsewhere, but all in natural ash (without the contrasting cream stripes) for a subtle change of pace. A double Planetaria mirror and wall lights in black steel, by Lara for Bohinc Studio, are mounted on the wall above.

BELOW In the downstairs WC, the walls are painted the same blue as the hallway. It looks so fresh and smart against the white marble wall panels designed by Lara with Serafini. On the wall is a single Planetaria mirror with a pair of wall lights in brushed brass and clear glass.

OPPOSITE The bathroom features a show-stopping marble shower area designed by Lara with Serafini and a freestanding tub by Bette. Natural light reflects off the shiny expanses of marble, glass and ceramic. Blush paint by Little Greene tones with the rosy hues of the marble and brings warmth to the room. At the window hangs a café curtain with a pretty bobble trim.

Everybody loves a narrowboat, right? Moored along a stretch of Regent's Canal in North West London, this wonderful boat speaks to my Romany heritage. On the day we visited, it was bathed in beautiful spring sunshine and I was captivated by its connection to a past way of life; it seemed to epitomize all the romance of a bygone era.

AFLOAT *in the City*

ABOVE RIGHT AND OPPOSITE **Stepping aboard this narrowboat, moored on a tree-lined stretch of canal, is almost like being transported into another world – it's easy to forget you're in the heart of London. Mat loves to sit in the bow of the boat, watching people walking up and down on the other side of the canal – what better way to pass a sunny evening? The statue with one of its arms missing was found discarded on the street.**

In 18th- and 19th-century Britain, narrowboats and the network of canals they navigated were crucial to the Industrial Revolution and still very much in use during the First World War. Originally drawn by horses and later powered by steam and then diesel, narrowboats were a key form of transport for raw materials and goods to and from the major shipping ports, markets and factories inland.

The boatmen and their families often lived onboard and life was hard, especially with the growth of the faster and more efficient rail network. During the mid 20th century, when much of the canal system was nationalized, many narrowboats fell into disrepair until gradually they became popular as houseboats and leisure boats.

The lucky person to call this piece of history his 'home on the water' is the positively charming Mat Whitley. Mat is the founder of Whitley London, suppliers of quality tailor-made suits at affordable prices. He was inspired to set up the business in 2013 after purchasing a bespoke 'whacky tweed' suit while on holiday in Tangier, Morocco. Mat and I first met a few years ago, when he was giving a creative talk to a class of students at one of the potential schools that my daughter Betty and I were looking around for her A levels. I found him such a gregarious, larger-than-life character and so full of fun that I simply had to stay in touch. I really wanted to include his fabulous floating home in this book, as it illustrates a unique way of living in the city.

Mat ended up on this boat by chance at a point in his life when he had nowhere to live. 'I suddenly remembered my mate had a canal boat. He said, "You're in luck, it's empty right now. I reckon you'll last a couple of weeks." That was 13 years ago, and now I simply can't imagine living anywhere else.'

It was not without its challenges, however. Mat says the boat looked very different when he first stepped aboard and since then he has completely transformed her. 'Living on a boat for the first time is a constant surprise.

There are so many hidden snags of which one has no conception – the loo, the shower, leaks, you name it!' Being so small, it also proved to be a less-than-ideal space to cohabit full time with another person, which he nevertheless managed to do for five years. 'It was impossible to get away from each other. And we lacked a walk-in wardrobe!' he adds with a laugh.

When deciding how to decorate and furnish the boat, his criteria were simple and traditional: 'Glossy, green and red.' It was also incredibly important for him to lay carpet, partly for comfort and warmth underfoot, but mainly because 'I didn't want it to be too "boaty" with that piney look.' When it comes to furnishings, inevitably a small space such as this can feel cluttered and he found reducing his 'stuff' to be extremely satisfying and cathartic. Most of the furniture and art are vintage pieces found at Golborne Road market. The look he was going for? 'Cheap, chic and cosy.'

One of the many joys of boat living is the freedom it offers. Mat can cast off and cruise the canals on a whim, but return to his permanent mooring when he pleases. 'I love taking my friends out on trips,' he says. 'It's a very different experience. Every time I return to the boat I get a little flutter of joy and excitement. I feel like a child on a glamorous camping holiday.'

OPPOSITE **I love kitchens with character and this little cooking area is no exception with its cheerful red cupboard doors and green-and-white checked curtains. Essentials, such as a coffee pot, corkscrew, clock and glasses, jostle for space with a fan, quirky figures and pictures by Piers Faccini, Anika Nixdorf and Alexander Beckett.**

BELOW LEFT **The bathroom fittings were chosen for their small size. I love the glossy black tiles decorated with silver stars and the picture of Marilyn Monroe. The gilt-framed mirror belonged to Mat's grandmother and the hanging garlands are from dear friends' memorial services.**

BELOW RIGHT **Looking from the matt white-painted kitchen into the bedroom, where a cosier colour palette prevails: deep red glossy paint on the walls and green carpet for warmth and comfort. A Chinese lantern and floral picture add to the eclectic feel.**

"I really wanted to include Mat's fabulous floating home in this book, as it illustrates a unique way of living in the city."

ABOVE In the seating area, a lamp from L'Isle-sur-la-Sorgue in Provence with a shade by Andrew St Clair sits on a mirrored chest of drawers/ dresser. The painting was from a gallery in Amsterdam.

RIGHT With a bed that takes up most of the width of the boat, Mat has created a cocooning space with a glossy green ceiling, deep red walls and layers of furnishings in rich tones. The bedside curtains are from an early 20th-century production by the Ballets Russes, while the large-scale floral drapes are from a market in Provence.

Entering this elegant five-storey Grade II-listed Georgian house in the Cotham area of Bristol feels like stepping back in time. Period features such as arches, columns, fanlights and fireplaces abound, and the rooms have the spacious, balanced proportions that are typical of the era, with high ceilings and generous-sized doorways and sash windows.

HISTORY *in the City*

OPPOSITE **The hall has its original staircase, panelling and cornicing/molding. The walls are painted in Farrow & Ball's Stony Ground, the woodwork/trim in French Gray and the floor and stairs in Mahogany. A colourful kilim from Nain Trading links the space with the study next door. To the left of the door is a mid-century Swiss vase, and above it is an 18th-century painted overmantel.**

ABOVE RIGHT **This statue is one of a pair by the garden pond. They depict two of the Three Graces, daughters of Zeus in Greek mythology, cast in concrete by the owner Catherine's late brother-in-law, sculptor Charles Mason.**

I first came across this amazing house when it was briefly put up for sale last year through Inigo, an estate agent specializing in the sale of exceptional historic homes. By the time I'd requested a viewing, it had been taken off the market for repairs, but it stayed in my mind and I'm so happy that its owner Catherine Mason allowed me to include it in this book.

This is a wonderful example of a house where the design and decoration have been carefully and sympathetically considered to enhance and preserve the original integrity of the building. At the same time, it is also a comfortable and welcoming home that reflects the personalities and stories of its inhabitants.

A notable feature of the interior is the row upon row of scholarly books that line almost every available wall space. It is not surprising to learn that the house has been the family home of academics for the past 45 years. It was bought in 1980, for the modest sum of £48,000, by Catherine's late husband Dr Tom Mason. It was a few years before they met, and Tom had moved to the area with his 11-year-old son to take up a position in the English department at the University of Bristol.

At the time, Catherine explains, Cotham was teetering between respectability and near slum: 'A few houses away, squatters were tearing up the floorboards of their upper storey and burning them to keep warm.' The house had been divided into flats and was very run-down, but it still had working fireplaces and original floorboards, windows, shutters, stairs, banisters and some panelling. Tom, whose literary specialism was the 17th and 18th centuries, had a particular appreciation of neoclassical and Palladian architecture, and a clear idea of what renovations would be in keeping with this early Georgian house. Gradually, he and his son repaired the interior together, floor by floor.

Catherine tells me that Tom, who died in 2022, had a particular fondness for secret rooms and cupboards, in which he hid away modern plumbing, radiators, WCs and computers.

He then attached large paintings to the doors to complete the disguise. 'It caused me a lot of trouble when I had to renovate parts of the house after his death,' she says with a smile.

The house and garden evolved over the years as the couple, who married in 1992, had what Catherine describes as 'a 30-year struggle' over furnishings. 'Tom's priorities were beauty, elegance and privacy, however impractical,' says Catherine. 'Mine, as the mother of two little children, were comfort, practicality and maximum sunshine in the garden.' Somehow they found a balance, although Catherine admits to having made a few sympathetic adaptations of her own in recent years.

In addition to the vast collection of books in English and German, the house is filled with art and artifacts. Tom grew up in a Swiss family in which art and literature were highly valued. His parents were Cambridge academics and many of the German tomes were inherited from his mother; the rest are Catherine's, whose late-career PhD (recently completed) is on the reception and decline of German literature in England since 1900.

Tom's grandfather Gottlieb Vest was a dental surgeon in Basel and a keen collector of art, from small Roman antiquities to modern Impressionist works. From local galleries, he had purchased works by artists including Henri Matisse, Paul Klee, René Victor Auberjonois, Bernard Buffet and Gabriel Zendel. Tom's brother Charles, who died in 2013, was also an artist and had lived in the house during his studies at the University of the West of England. Many of the modern sculptures are his works.

Catherine says the house is especially loved by the friends of her now-adult children, who have known it all their lives. Even though they may be unfamiliar with the works of all these great authors and artists, they still feel at home among them. For her part, she loves that it represents 'a faded English and European culture that was so widely valued by previous generations'. It's a magical house steeped in history, which connects us to a bygone age.

OPPOSITE AND ABOVE **The light-filled modern extension, used as a reading room, opens onto the leafy garden. A green Persian Gabbeh rug, topped with a kilim, seems to bring the outdoors in. Through the archway is the study and classics library. The panelling is painted in Farrow & Ball's Picture Gallery Red, while the vaulted ceiling has been finished with Imperial Gold by Charles Roberson Liquid Metal. The framed engraving is *Tenant's Family* (1795) by Charles Knight, one of a pair with *Landord's Family* (not seen), which conceals the door leading into the downstairs cloakroom. Above the secret door is a bronze statue of the Swiss poet Carl Spitteler.**

ABOVE The garden room leads to both the study, through the arch on the right, and the hall, through the mirrored double doors. Along the back wall of the bookcase are a series of mirrored doors, which can be closed to conceal the middle row of books and also to reflect the light and views of the garden.

OPPOSITE The huge glass bay window curves up into an overhead fanlight, to provide maximum daylight above the Swiss Biedermeier writing desk that faces the garden. Sitting here, in the cane-backed chair, must be the most perfect place to write. The statue of a recumbent female figure is by Charles Mason.

PAGES 178–179 The shelving on the right of the garden room was built to house the many antiquarian books, from Chaucer to Alexander Pope, as well as the German and Latin library inherited from Tom's parents. The teak coffee table is a 1960s piece by Kai Kristiansen, while the yellow armchairs are from Wayfair.

Degas
LEONARDO DA VINCI
REMBRANDT
SANDRO BOTTICELLI
RAPHAEL

CRANACH
The Bible and its Painters
SANDRO BOTTICELLI

OPPOSITE The front drawing room houses the library of 18th- to 20th-century volumes and modern German literature in shelving built by Tom and painted in French Gray by Farrow & Ball. This is a great neutral that works well with all the other tones of brown, red, ochre and green. The much-loved vintage armchair, next to the mahogany revolving bookcase, is another cosy place to read.

ABOVE LEFT The house is full of intriguing details, such as this sculptured niche with an inset painted plaster bas-relief by Charles Mason with Roman figurines below.

LEFT I love how, interspersed among the plethora of wonderful old volumes that bring a lived-in feel to this house, the shelving is used to display sculptures and fascinating artifacts, such as this marble head and the figurine behind it by Charles Mason.

ABOVE The original archway at the foot of the staircase frames the view from the inner hall into the stone-flagged outer hall. The palette is beautifully balanced, with the warm tones underfoot offset by the sophisticated combination of Farrow & Ball's Stony Ground walls and French Gray doors and panelling.

ABOVE **The same subtle colour palette is continued through to the landing and corridor upstairs, where there hangs a copy of a drawing by Henri Matisse called *Head of a Woman*. The original was acquired by Tom's Swiss grandfather Gottlieb Vest and is now owned by his great-grandson Jack.**

RIGHT **The bedroom floor and walls are painted in understated Cornforth White by Farrow & Ball, with hints of colour introduced by the bedspread, books and art. The sculpture above the original fireplace is by Charles Mason, while the paintings and lithographs disguising the cupboards are by Gabriel Zendel.**

THE GOLDEN
ANNUAL FOR GIRLS
THE MECHANISED IMAGE
GILLIAN TINDALL
LEOPARD VI

OPPOSITE AND RIGHT **Another bedroom with a wonderful original fireplace and cupboards and shelving built by Tom. Above the corner cupboard hangs a painting of a blossoming tree by Gabriel Zendel, while reflected in the gilt-framed mirror is a pair of 19th-century Chinese prints of a courtesan. Entry to the room is through a secret door constructed by Tom and disguised by a niche containing a Roman bronze statuette of Priapus, a fertility god in Greek mythology. On the wall to the left of the door are two drawings, in pen and gold ink, of scenes from Ovid's *Metamorphoses* by W. Collin.**

"The design and decoration have been carefully and sympathetically considered to enhance and preserve the original integrity of the building."

RESOURCES AND SUPPLIERS

Pearl Lowe
www.pearllowe.co.uk
IG: @pearllowe and
@pearllowevintage

ANTIQUES & VINTAGE

Brocante Living
www.brocanteliving.co.uk
IG: @amybrocante_living

Coach House Brocante
www.coachhousebrocante.com
IG: @coachhousebrocante

Cosy Dot Company
www.cosy.company
IG: @cosydotcompany

Dairy House Vintage & Home
www.dairyhouseantiques.com
IG: @dairyhouseantiques

Dean Antiques
www.deanantiques.co.uk
IG: @deanantiques

Dora Gray Designs
www.doragraydesigns.co.uk
IG: @doragraydesigns

Hand of Glory
www.handofgloryantiques.com
+44 (0)7867 305451
IG: @handofgloryantiques

Hoof Brocante
IG: @hoof.antiques_brocante

Ibbi
www.ibbidirect.co.uk
IG: @ibbi_interiors

Ivy Joan
www.ivyjoan.co.uk
IG: @brocanteivyjoan

Jasper Jacks
www.jasperjacks.com

Lark Vintage
www.larkvintage.co.uk
IG: @larkvintage

Les Couilles du Chien
www.lescouillesduchien.com
IG: @les_couilles_du_chien

Little White Cat Decorative
IG: @littlewhitecatdecorative

Marchand Antiques
www.marchandantiques.co.uk
IG: @marchand_antiques

Mason and Painter
IG: @masonandpainter

Merchant 57
IG: @hastingsmerchant57

My Nook Shop
IG: @mynookshop

No.4 Vintage
www.no4vintage.com
IG: @no.4vintage

Old Albion
www.oldalbion.co.uk
IG: @oldalbion

Old Stock Antiques
www.oldstockantiques.co.uk
IG: @oldstockantiques

Out of the Attic
www.outoftheattic.uk
IG: @outof_theattic

P&T Antiques
www.pt-antiques.co.uk
IG: @pt_antiques

Rag & Bone
www.ragandbonebristol.com
IG: @ragandbonebristol

Tapissage
IG: @tapissage

Tara Franklin Antiques
IG: @tara.franklin_antiques

Textile Trunk
www.textiletrunk.com
IG: @textiletrunk

The Antique Kitchen
www.theantiquekitchen.co.uk
@theantiquekitchen

The Curious Flea
IG: @Thecuriousflea

The French Depot
www.thefrenchdepot.com
IG: @thefrenchdepot

The French House
www.thefrenchhouse.co.uk
IG: @thefrenchhouseyork

Three Angels
www.threeangelsbrighton.com
IG: @threeangelshove_lifestyle

Trove 1489
IG: @trove1489

Urban Raid Trading
IG: @urbanraidtrading

Vintage on the Vine
www.vintageonthevine.co.uk
IG: @vintageonthevine

Vintage at the vicarage
www.vintageatthevicarage.co.uk
IG: @vintage_at_the_vicarage

RECLAMATION & SALVAGE

Frome Reclamation
www.fromerec.co.uk

Glastonbury Reclamation
www.glastonburyreclamation.co.uk

LASSCO
www.lassco.co.uk

Retrouvius
www.retrouvius.com

Salvo
www.salvoweb.com

Symonds Salvage
www.symondssalvage.co.uk

Wells Reclamation
www.wellsreclamation.com

FURNITURE, LIGHTING & ACCESSORIES

Baileys Home
www.baileyshome.com
IG: @baileyshome

Beauvamp
www.beauvamp.com
IG: @beauvamp

Graham and Green
www.grahamandgreen.co.uk
IG @grahamandgreen

House of Hackney
www.houseofhackney.com
IG @houseofhackney

Penhaligon's
www.penhaligons.com
IG: @penhaligons

Preen by Thornton Bregazzi
www.preenbythorntonbregazzi.com
IG: @preenhome

Rachel Ashwell – Shabby Chic
www.shabbychic.com
IG: @officialshabbychic

Rae
raelifestyle.com
IG: @rae_lifestyle_

Rothschild & Bickers
www.rothschildbickers.com
@rothschildbickers

Sera of London
www.seraoflondon.com
IG: @seraoflondon

SHOP
IG: @shopnormanroad

Soho Home
www.sohohome.com
IG: @sohohome

The Stripes Company
www.thestripescompany.com
IG: @thestripescompany

Toast
www.toa.st
+44 (0)333 400 5200
IG: @toast

Trash Velvet
www.trashvelvet.co.uk
IG @trashvelvetuk

KITCHENS & BATHROOMS

BC Designs
www.bcdesigns.co.uk
IG: @bcdesignsuk

Bert & May
www.bertandmay.com
IG: @bertandmay

DeVol
www.devolkitchens.co.uk
IG: @devolkitchens

Swan
shop.swan-brand.co.uk
IG: @swanbranduk

WALLPAPER, PAINT, TEXTILES & TRIMMINGS

Benjamin Moore
www.benjaminmoorepaint.co.uk
IG: @benjaminmooreuk

Coco & Wolf
cocoandwolf.co.uk
IG: @cocoandwolf

Farrow & Ball
www.farrow-ball.com
IG: @farrowandball

Francesca's Paints
francescaspaint.com
IG: @francescaspaintsltd

Jean Monro
www.jeanmonro.com
IG: @jeanmonroprints

Liberty
www.libertyfabric.com
IG: @libertyhomeandinteriors

Morris & Co
www.wmorrisandco.com
IG: @wmorrisandco

Mulberry Home
IG: @mulberry_home

Piglet in Bed
www.pigletinbed.com
IG: @pigletinbed

Samuel & Sons
www.samuelandsons.com
IG @samuelandsons

Soak & Sleep
www.soakandsleep.com
+44 (0)1483 616616
IG: @soakandsleep

Society of Wanderers
www.societyofwanderers.com
IG: @societyofwanderers

The Cloth Shop
www.theclothshop.net
IG: @clothshoplondon

Tori Murphy
www.torimurphy.com
IG: @torimurphytextiles

VV Rouleaux
www.vvrouleaux.com
IG: @vvrouleaux

CARPETS & RUGS

Frances Loom
www.francesloom.com
IG: @francesloom

Roger Oates Design
www.rogeroates.com
IG: @roger_oates

Wendy Morrison Design
www.wendymorrisondesign.com
IG @wendymorrisondesign

PARASOLS

East London Parasol Company
eastlondonparasols.com
IG: @eastlondonparasolco

Sunbeam Jackie
www.sunbeamjackie.com
IG: @sunbeam_jackie

FLOWERS

Scarlet & Violet
www.scarletandviolet.com
IG: @scarletandviolet

The Witham Flowery
IG: @the_witham_flowery

Wild at Heart
www.wildatheart.com
IG: @wildatheartheq

PICTURE CREDITS

All photography by Kate Martin unless otherwise stated.

Key: *Ph* = photographer

1–3 The home of designer and author Pearl Lowe in West London; **4 left** The London home of artist and designer Susi Bellamy; **4 centre** The home of Heather Alston and architect Dominic Warren; **4 right** The London home of artist and designer Susi Bellamy; **5 left** The home of designer and author Pearl Lowe in West London; **5 centre** The London home of artist and designer Susi Bellamy; **5 right** The home of designer and author Pearl Lowe in West London; **6–11** Muirshin Durkin in Notting Hill; **12–31** The home of designer and author Pearl Lowe in West London; **32–49** The home of Heather Alston and architect Dominic Warren; **50–67** The London home of artist and designer Susi Bellamy; **68–81** Azzi Glasser, perfumer, perfume designer and founder of The Perfumer's Story; **82–99** The home, shops and studio of designer Solange Azagury-Partridge; **100–115** The London family home of vintage curator Carmen Haid; **116–131** *Ph* © Helena Christensen, The home of photographer and model Helena Christensen in New York City; **132–149** The London studio of artist Jonathan Yeo, www.jonathanyeo.com; **150–165** Lunar House, the London home of designer Lara Bohinc and her family; **166–171** Mat Whitley of Whitley London and Medium Rare; **172–185** The house of Catherine Mason in Cotham, Bristol; **187** Lunar House, the London home of designer Lara Bohinc and her family; **188** The home of designer and author Pearl Lowe in West London; **191** The London studio of artist Jonathan Yeo, www.jonathanyeo.com; **192** The home of designer and author Pearl Lowe in West London.

BUSINESS CREDITS

Pearl Lowe
Designer and author
www.pearllowe.co.uk
IG: @pearllowe
Pages 1–3, 5 left and right, 12–31, 188 and 192.

Susi Bellamy
Artist and designer
www.susi-bellamy.com

Interior design in collaboration with
Pandora Taylor
www.pandorataylor.co.uk
Pages 4 left and right, 5 centre and 50–67.

Heather Alston and Dominic Warren

Kate Forman Designs Ltd
www.kateforman.co.uk

Douglas Watson Studio
Bespoke handprinted tiles
www.douglaswatsonstudio.uk
Pages 4 centre and 32–49.

Muirshin Durkin
Antiques and vintage
www.muirshindurkin.co.uk
Pages 6–11.

Azzi Glasser
Perfumer and perfume designer

The Perfumer's Story by Azzi
www.theperfumersstory.com
Pages 68–81.

Carmen Haid

Atelier Mayer
www.atelier-mayer.com

Olivier Mourao
Artist
IG: @oliviermourao.art

Danny Lane
Artist
IG: @dannylanesculpture
Pages 100–115.

Jonathan Yeo
Artist
www.jonathanyeo.com

Spiral staircase fabricated by
Metal Works London
www.metalworkslondon.com
Pages 132–149 and 191.

Lara Bohinc
Designer

Bohinc Studio
www.bohincstudio.com
Pages 150–165.

Mat Whitley

Whitley London
www.whitley.london

Medium Rare
www.mediumrare.tv
Pages 166–171.

Catherine Mason

Catherine's home is the subject of an interior still-life oil painting by
Eleanor Crow
Artist
www.eleanorcrow.org
Pages 172–185.

INDEX

Page numbers in *italics* refer to the illustrations and their captions

SKOG
500 PORTRAITS
Saul Bass
Philip Guston
MICHAEL BORREMANS
KIPPENBERGER
JONATHAN YEO
MAGRITTE
IN THE FLESH
Breakfast with Lucian
Georges Braque

ACKNOWLEDGMENTS

I would like to thank my Mum and her partner Pat for helping us bring magic to our sweet little abode. A special thank you to Mauricio and his team for all their hard work.

Thank you to Kate Martin for making everything look so incredibly beautiful, and to Alex Teal for adding pure magic to every place we photographed. Thank you to Leslie Harrington and Annabel Morgan for believing in me so that I could create another book. Thanks to Sophie Devlin for her help in completing the book.

A massive thank you to, Toni Kay, Patricia Harrington, Yvonne Doolan, Zia Mattocks, Hope Coke, Zoe Tennant, Alannah Newnham, Hannah Gourley and all at Platform Creative. It's been a dream working with you all!

Finally, thank you to the homeowners for welcoming us into your enchanting spaces. This book would not have been possible without all of you.